Exploring Research Data Management

Exploring Research Data Management

Andrew M. Cox and Eddy Verbaan

facet
publishing

© Andrew Cox and Eddy Verbaan 2018

Published by Facet Publishing
7 Ridgmount Street, London WC1E 7AE
www.facetpublishing.co.uk

Facet Publishing is wholly owned by CILIP:
the Library and Information Association.

The authors have asserted their right under the Copyright, Designs and Patents Act 1988 to be identified as authors of this work.

British Library Cataloguing in Publication Data
A catalogue record for this book is available from the British Library.

ISBN 978-1-78330-278-9 (paperback)
ISBN 978-1-78330-279-6 (hardback)
ISBN 978-1-78330-280-2 (e-book)

First published 2018

Text printed on FSC accredited material.

FSC
MIX
Paper from
responsible sources
FSC® C013604
www.fsc.org

Cover design by Kathryn Beecroft
Typeset from author's files in 11/14pt Revival 565 and Frutiger by Flagholme Publishing Services.
Printed and made in Great Britain by CPI Group (UK) Ltd, Croydon, CR0 4YY.

Contents

List of tables and figures

Tables

Figures

CHAPTER 1

Introducing research data management

Aims

The aims of this chapter are to:

- introduce the topic of research data management (RDM) and what it means in practice
- explain the thinking behind the book, so you can use it effectively.

A thought experiment

Imagine going to a busy researcher's office:

- What would you expect to see?

And if you asked them about their research history:

- What would their story be like?

And if you asked them specifically about the 'data' that they collect as part of their research:

- What types of data would they say they have?
- How much data would they have?
- How would they store and back up their data?
- Who would they say owns the data?
- Would they say they share the data with others, or not?

Let's offer an answer based on the answers of one of the authors of this book (himself a researcher). Andrew says:

Well, I am embarrassed to say my office is pretty untidy: a table strewn with papers; three bookshelves packed with books, reports, print-outs – a lot relating to research, but also teaching. A filing cabinet, which if you unlock it, is jam-packed with various papers, including some things like hand-drawn maps of an area of Sheffield; a stack of completed questionnaires; a roll of flipchart paper covered with Post-it notes, from a data collection workshop last year. All that is stuff I have gathered for my research. There are quite a few folders of interview transcripts as well. Some go way back! Also in there are some old-looking memory sticks. I wonder what's on them myself!

Of course where I work most of the time is here at the computer. Again, it's going to be hard for me to summarise what is on the computer. Here is a secure network drive where I keep a lot of project work – or used to – alongside files relating to teaching. The university also has a secure Google drive service. There is also a research data server. I guess I basically keep material in folders by project. But quite often it's a bit more complicated than that. For example, I might re-use material across a number of projects.

As regards my research journey, I have been working here for about 10 years. In that time I have participated in I don't know how many different projects. They are clustered around a few areas where I have really had an ongoing fascination, e.g. RDM itself, but also experiences of library space. And quite a lot relating to various social media research projects I have done. Quite a few projects were one-off, just pursuing an interest I had at the time. There are some projects where I worked on my own. Often with a research assistant who collected and maybe analysed some of the data. In other cases it was part of a much larger project that was funded, had a number of partners and where we shared various tasks, including gathering and analysing data. There was also PhD students' work where they were the lead and I supported them through the research process. But even at the current moment I am working on at least a dozen projects at once! That is excluding PhD student and Masters dissertation work, both of which also involve original data collection.

In terms of data, as I am a qualitative researcher, so I have lots of interview recordings and resulting transcripts. I have also done quite a lot with visual data like photographs, hand-drawn maps and diagrams. I have also done work through questionnaires, be that printed or online. Hence lots of Excel and SPSS files.

I really have no idea how much data I have in gigabytes! Probably not that much but there are a lot of different files. Here is one we are working on now: there are 30 interview recordings and the same number of transcripts. There is an Nvivo file for it. There are also related Excel spreadsheets from our questionnaire. It could all quite easily fit on a memory stick, but it's a lot of stuff in a large number of files.

Stuff is backed up mostly on the university servers, but via a number of pots, such as my personal university drive (but that is pretty full!). In the last couple of years the university cloud storage has come in. At first I must admit I didn't like it, but now I'm using it more and more both for day-to-day sharing of project documents like plans and the data we have gathered. There is also a specific research data server which the computer service has just set up for my research group. I'm just starting to use that too. Plus, of course, any print-outs, etc., in the filing cabinet, or a locked drawer of my desk.

I kind of realise that the university legally owns the data, but it's me that cares about it and uses it.

In the past there has not been so much data sharing; but things are changing. We just shared data from a survey about bibliometrics on the university data repository. We have also shared data related to publications. I'm in favour of data sharing, but in reality we have only begun to get into the habit of sharing data. If I'm honest I'm doubtful if most of it would be much use to another researcher, as it's very specific to my project. Equally I haven't myself re-used data created by another researcher – though that is a very appealing idea!

Maybe you imagined something very different. That does not mean you are wrong. One of the most significant features of RDM is that we cannot easily generalise across different researchers' behaviour.

The answers Andrew gave are probably not untypical for a qualitative social scientist. Such researchers have lots of data files, of a variety of types, from many projects, but it is not 'big data'. They store the data in various places. They have a lot of stuff, which is managed in a rather ad hoc way – sometimes off university servers. Sharing research data is a fairly new idea.

A researcher in another discipline might have a very different experience. They could be generating massive quantities of data through complex, multi-million dollar collaborative research projects. This could throw up a very different set of issues.

Exploring further

Thinking about this situation one can begin to see there are a number of potential problems in Andrew's behaviour, attitudes and expectations. RDM is precisely about making the management of data more effective.

Spend some time re-reading the text above and identify some of the potential issues that Andrew's habits create for him.

RDM

Research data management (RDM) is about creating, finding, organising, storing, sharing and preserving data within any research process.

Improving how research data are managed day to day, and particularly promoting its sharing and re-use, has the potential to increase the richness and reliability of research.

Thinking of Andrew's experience we can identify a number of issues that Andrew has:

- He doesn't have big data but he does have a lot of different types of data, of varying types – how is he going to manage this data more effectively so he can be sure to find material himself in the future?
- Even if he can find the data file again, will he be able to remember its context? Is it adequately documented?
- Within his collaborative projects, is he managing access to live data securely?
- Some of this data appears to need keeping beyond the length of the project – is this being done securely where appropriate?
- How can Andrew be motivated to prepare his data so others can re-use it for other research?
- How can he be helped to re-use data that has already been collected?

All these issues create potential problems around day-to-day management of data, file storage and security, sharing and re-using of data.

This thought experiment gives us a first insight into the kinds of problem that research data management deals with: how to help researchers manage their data much better, for their own good, but also for the wider benefit of research. We can see that it's a complex area, where there are a host of potential problems that people might need help

Exploring further

Perhaps you have a friend who does research. If you have, go and ask them some of the questions we have discussed above. Or find a friendly researcher to chat to over a cup of coffee.

This is the first step of your journey into getting to grips with the issues around research data management. Getting a deeper understanding of what they actually do is going to be invaluable for getting a feel for what their issues are and how they will respond to initiatives you might want to launch around RDM.

with but which has to engage with the extreme individuality of research in different areas.

Why is RDM important now?

This issue of managing research data has become a key issue now, driven by a number of factors. Firstly, the 'deluge of data' arising from new types of science, a crisis in confidence in research integrity in certain fields and the general movement for open data have led to increasing concerns around managing data better and sharing it more. Many funders around the world now require that researchers plan this much better. Also to get their articles accepted by journals researchers increasingly need to publish the data on which their results are based. In response many universities (and other research organisations) have set up institutional research data policies, training and advice services, and perhaps a repository or catalogue describing institutional data holdings. Typically research data services are being developed within universities, led by people from computing services, libraries and/or research administration.

This book is for people who want to get involved in supporting RDM in such ways. It may not sound so hard to do this, but it is about managing a change in how researchers do things day to day, fitting the needs of specific institutions and its wider policies, but also changing longstanding cultures in research fields, in a context of changing technologies. So it is a major professional challenge for those who support improvement in RDM.

Exploring further

Do some desk research to find out what is going on in your own institution, be that where you work or where you are studying.

- Is there a policy relating to research data? If so, what does it say, and how does it fit into the wider structures of research governance? Can you work out where leadership for RDM sits?
- Is there a website for RDM? Who runs it?
- What training is being offered?
- Is there a data repository? What type of material is stored there?

Looking for this kind of material will begin to give you an idea of how institutions are supporting researchers to improve their RDM.

What does the practice of supporting RDM actually involve?

Another immediate way of trying to understand what RDM is about is thinking about the kind of questions professionals supporting RDM might be asked. It could be things like:

- How can I locate data for re-use in my research?
- How do I complete a data management plan for a research proposal for a particular funder?
- I want to share data with a project partner at another institution. Where should I store research data to share it securely?
- Where is the best place to store my data for long-term preservation?
- How would I cite someone else's data in my journal article?

These are actually quite complex questions. For example, where a researcher might find data for a particular project is, obviously, highly dependent on their specific research questions. Similarly, different funders have very different views on what a data management plan should contain. Local arrangements for active data storage and sharing and data preservation are very specific.

Exploring further

Pick one or two of the questions above and start exploring on the web to see if you can find material for an answer. The answer might be in online resources, provided at an institutional or national level. Or it might be to refer to a local expert who knows the answer. But obviously knowing who is who is as important as knowing the answer yourself.

Who is this book for?

This book is for anyone interested in building their understanding of RDM, particularly in a university context. Your background could be in:

- libraries, because librarians have many relevant skills in training and advice, metadata creation
- computing, because there are many technical issues around the storage of active and archival data
- archives and records management, because archivists are particularly interested in aspects of preservation of any kind of data that is produced

- research administration, because many of the issues link to the wider governance of research, including research integrity and relations with funders of research
- research itself, because many of the issues around RDM relate to understanding the motivations and methods of research.

Or your background could be in something else. We do not assume a particular professional background or prior knowledge in this book.

You could be a student in one of these fields. We have not assumed you already have a specific role. If you work at a particular institution you will often want to explore further within your own organisation or comparable ones. If you are a student it probably makes sense to identify one or two institutions that interest you and consistently work on exploring your understanding of that institution through the activities in the book. That will give you a more holistic viewpoint.

If you are thinking of working in this area you will be looking out for adverts for jobs with titles such as:

- RDM co-ordinator
- Data librarian
- Data curator
- Research data service officer/assistant
- Research data metadata specialist.

Some are more specialist than others, but by reading the book you will gain a much clearer idea of the subtle differences in role and where your skills might take you.

On the other hand you may have no intention of directly being involved in such dedicated RDM roles, but realise it is of relevance to you more indirectly. For example, it may simply be an aspect of appreciating the wider context within which you work. This book is intended to be a good place to start to grasp the dimensions of RDM and how it might touch your current role.

About the book

Research data management is not the most exciting-sounding term. But we think this is a really fascinating area of professional work. It's fairly new, so the answers are not well understood. No one size fits all organisations, so professionals working in this area need to work out how general principles fit their institution. In the book we want to stimulate your curiosity, enterprise and creativity in working out solutions to complex problems for all sorts of researchers based in all sorts of institutions. So the book is not a dry reference work full of largely unexplained acronyms or an insider account for other insiders. It briefs you succinctly and engagingly on the main issues. It combines this grounding with many quotes, stories and case studies, diagrams, ideas and provocations, together with tasks to undertake to make learning about RDM thought-provoking and stimulating.

We have included a lot of 'Exploring further' sections, because to really learn about RDM you will need to get out there, find out more about specific organisations and research cultures, and start talking to people. RDM is not a solved problem. It's complex, particularly the challenges around influencing longstanding research cultures. The support needs of different academic disciplines are very different. And the challenges vary between institutions, too. This book is the starting point for you to open up a positive dialogue for partnership with researchers, in order to develop research data services (RDS) suitable for a specific context. We have used many of the activities in workshops about RDM, and they work well as collective exercises. You may want to share your voyage of discovery with others, or use them in cascading your understanding to colleagues.

Much of the book is based on the authors' own experiences of trying to understand RDM and develop services in their context. We also worked together on the RDMRose project, which developed a set of training materials on RDM (specifically for librarians, but generically useful). We have also published a number of pieces of research work that inform the

Exploring further

If you are working in an institution already, find out who is involved in RDM in organisations local to yours; drop them an e-mail, introducing yourself and inviting them for coffee. Find out if there is a local professional interest group around RDM in your area. Our experience is that this community will be helpful. Also look online for groups that you can join who discuss RDM.

If you are a student, look at the RDM website for a number of institutions of different types in your region. Does this reveal major differences in how RDM is viewed and prioritised? Which website do you think is most effective and why? We will look a lot more closely at RDM websites in Chapter 11.

book. It is also based on reflecting on our personal experiences as researchers. Andrew has a PhD in information science, Eddy in history.

Yet we would not want to say this book is highly original; rather, it's more a distillation of knowledge gained from talking to people working on RDM over the last five years. Our aim was to capture something of their values, skills and ways of thinking and talking. As such it should help you to understand how you can fit into and contribute to this world.

Further reading

While far from comprehensive, Bailey's rolling *Research Data Curation Bibliography* (2017) is a good starting point for getting a feel for the literature around RDM. Some searches, such as for keywords you are interested in, will give you a feel for some of the main writings around a particular topic. Searching by date will give you a feel for what people are writing about at the moment.

Bailey, C. W. (2017) *Research Data Curation Bibliography*, http://digital-scholarship.org/rdcb/rdcb.htm.

CHAPTER 2

The social worlds of research

Aims

The aim of this chapter is to prompt you to reflect on the nature of research. By definition, if we are going to support RDM, we need to have some understanding of the intellectual and social organisation of research.

Introduction

If you come from an academic library background you may well have been attracted to the profession by an enthusiasm for information literacy. Libraries have made huge strides in the last few years towards making a very strong contribution to teaching in universities. Now we seem to be seeing a turn towards more support to research. Something of the same trend seems to be happening in IT services. In this context it is useful to reflect more on the current research landscape. You may work in research administration, in which case much of this will be familiar, but it is worth stepping back and reflecting on one's assumptions about research.

Exploring further

Jot down some keywords that describe 'research' as an idea. Then do some work trying to think how these might link through to RDM.

The research landscape

Research is a central activity for many universities. It is a key source of revenue: a multi-billion dollar business. Ideologically it is core to many university missions: particularly in 'research-intensive', elite institutions it is really what defines their special status.

Some key features of research you might have thought of earlier are:

- Funding – the competitive struggle to gain funding for research is central to many researchers' lives. Gaining a grant means having the resources to do bigger scale work and come up with more significant findings. Thus the positon of funders on RDM is critical. Nevertheless, it should be remembered that much research is still unfunded, or perhaps more accurately funded by institutions themselves through the time they give academic staff to do research.

• Projects – a lot of research, similarly to professional support work, is organised in projects. This colours a lot of research-related behaviour, e.g. it shows up in how people store their personal files. Thus, they are fixed-funded for a limited time period with fairly clear deliverables. This has consequences for RDM in terms of what happens when the project finishes. At project end there may be no resources for doing work on sharing data.

• Publication – the ultimate aim of academics is typically to produce a peer-reviewed publication, be that a journal article, conference paper or a book. Research data are the foundation of the findings, but it is not always seen as a valid output in itself. This may affect RDM in terms of the motivation to publish data: for one thing, the infra-structure for finding, sharing and citing data is much less familiar than that for publishing outputs. The institutional and peer recognition that comes from data sharing may be far less than for publishing results.

• Big science – a significant amount of research takes place in multi-million dollar projects, involving expensive equipment. Such projects may generate huge amounts of data.

• Collaboration – funders favour collaborative work. They increasingly want work that solves real-world problems, which implies collaboration of multiple experts, because it gives the scale of resource to explore a problem and a range of different expertise.

• Interdisciplinarity – as well as collaboration between researchers there is often an interest by funders in greater working across established disciplinary boundaries. By combining expertise from different subjects it is more likely to be possible to come up with innovative solutions.

• Social impact – funders increasingly value research that has a benefit to society, be that through directly addressing urgent social problems or stimulating economic growth.

• The terms 'Mode 1' and 'Mode 2' knowledge creation contrast two ways science can work. Mode 1 is a more traditional model of the individual scholar seeking to answer questions for their own sake.

Mode 2 summarises many of the changes we have already mentioned towards short-term, project-based, interdisciplinary collaborations to solve a specific societal problem in a particular domain of application. The shift to Mode 2 is seen as driven by funding priorities.

- Digital scholarship – can refer to a wide range of new and not-so-new behaviours, but it points to more networked researchers who work together in more informal ways.
- Research-led teaching and undergraduate research – in a complex world, it is increasingly thought that everyone needs to have some of the capabilities of a researcher, such as gathering data about a problem in a systematic way. Research-led teaching refers to teaching that might encompass the latest research results, but could also imply students learning by themselves doing research. Even undergraduate curriculums could have a strong element of undertaking a small-scale research project. The implication is that for students, too, RDM issues become important. For example, if they are doing interviews they need to plan the secure storage of the outcome.
- New Public Management/neo-liberalisation – refers to the increasing application of private sector management strategies to universities. This implies greater talk about customer needs, increasing reliance on metrics of performance such as funding and citation counting. This perceived trend to the greater management pressures on academics is tied to a loss of status and even an identity crisis for the academic profession. It is important to consider this context, because RDM can itself be seen as 'yet another' form of such control. Maybe it is sometimes. It can also be something very positive for researchers, too; how we position RDM therefore becomes critical to how it is perceived.

The organisation of research

The organisation of research: meta-disciplines, academic tribes and sub-fields.

It is common to talk about fundamental differences in culture between meta-disciplines, such as:

- pure science
- life sciences
- applied sciences
- social science

- arts and humanities.

It is fairly common to think that the response to RDM is somewhat different in these different areas of research. Stereotypically the individualist humanities scholar rejects the very term data. Applied scientists already share data intensively. Of course, this is a simplification, but it may help to suggest some rather fundamental divergences across academic research.

But such a high-level categorisation neglects differences between, say, historians, linguists and philosophers. So going down one level it may be useful to look at individual subject fields or disciplines. Becher and Trowler's (2001) notion that disciplines are global 'academic tribes' has been very influential in our understanding of research. In a sense, academics identify more with this tribe than with the institution that employs them. This is analogous to a professional's loyalty to wider professional values, but is probably stronger than in many professions. It means that academics may be more alert to trends around RDM in their academic network than to anything the institution may wish to promote.

The idea of the academic tribe draws attention to the way that scholars operate in unique and diverse social worlds, sharing a sense of:

- the scope of the field of study and where its boundaries lie
- the subject's history (and shared myths)
- a conception of what is a 'contribution to knowledge', i.e. what counts as new
- methodological commitments e.g. what are 'normal' ways of doing science, such as collecting and analysing data in certain types of ways certain institutions, such as key research centres
- key figures, such as seminal authors and rising stars
- formal communication channels: journals and conferences that are key to a field – academics tend to have a strong view of where it is best to publish
- social networks, with gatekeepers – the famous 'invisible college'
- vocabularies and ways of talking, thinking and acting
- identity and personal commitment to this community.

The logic of this perspective is that RDM will look different to different academic tribes. Some will already have been doing it well for years; others have no notion even of data. For the RDM professional based in an institution this is a key challenge, because the researcher's strongest loyalties are invested in a world beyond the institution, where institutional action cannot easily reach. The challenge thus is to change a culture that has its roots elsewhere. Much of the literature on RDM, for example, reflects the variation of definitions of data and practices of sharing across disciplines (Borgman, 2015).

If anything this picture is actually too simplistic. The notion of a tribe implies a rather coherent sub-culture or community. In fact, scholars within one field may have little in common with others working in a different speciality. Some forms of sociology are very theoretical; some are based on secondary analysis of quantitative data. The feel of the subject is very different. Perhaps the most extreme example is geography, where some geographers are natural scientists studying landforms while others are essentially social theorists.

Furthermore, it is increasingly understood that 'research tracks and specialties grow, split, join, adapt and die' as Klein (1996, 55) puts it. If you work in a library, think about the way that the titles of journals change quite rapidly to reflect fashions in thinking. New journals emerge to reflect new disciplinary combinations. In a material form these changes reflect shifting currents in academic thinking. Various flavours of interdisciplinarity and multidisciplinarity reshape the research landscape continuously. This implies a less monolithic picture than implied by a focus on discipline or academic tribe. Perhaps the level of analysis should be one sub-field or speciality, since it is only at this level that a coherent value system still exists.

Exploring further

Do some web-based investigation of an area of research of interest to you. You might want to look at a specific department in the institution where you work or study. What meta-discipline does it fall under? Where does it fit into the map of academic disciplines? What specialities make it up? You will begin to see the complexity. Thus even along one corridor the range of specialities represented can be quite huge.

Narrowing down to a particular speciality, can you get a feel for the main journals and conferences and the key figures? What research methods are in use?

You might want to go on and start to explore research data practices as such: is there a subject repository for this area? Do people share data?

The individuality of research fields is marked.

Understanding something of this is critical to RDM because the message is likely to be very different for different fields.

The research lifecycle

A common way of thinking about research is through the notion of the research process or perhaps lifecycle. In the very broadest terms research moves from a stage of ideation, to funding, to permission, to data collection, to data analysis and then to write-up and further dissemination. Quite commonly one project leads to another that develops the ideas further, and in that sense it could be seen as a renewing lifecycle.

Actual research processes are pretty different. If you look at a research methods book and compare qualitative, quantitative and mixed-method research, the designs are typically different. Qualitative research, in particular, is usually seen as defying simple description. It's non-linear, iterative, variable.

Exploring further

Continue the work from the previous activity: start looking at a research methods book for a particular speciality. What are the range of methods in use? What kinds of data are being created?

If you get a chance to go to a research seminar from that area or to talk to a researcher, try and start to open up a conversation about the nature of the research community.

The experience of research: research and identity

Research is a very particular type of work. For many researchers it is a personal passion. They think about it over many years, care deeply about the issues at stake and invest huge amounts of time and energy in it. It is certainly tightly linked to their own sense of identity. When we think about RDM we need to bear in mind this strong personal investment that many researchers make in their research.

One useful perspective for thinking about this a little more systematically is to refer to Brew's work on the experience of research (Brew, 2001). Rather than focusing on differences by discipline, her findings pointed to four main types of experience of research across all disciplines.

1   The **domino conception**, in which research is seen as an ordered process in which different atomistic elements are synthesised.

2   The **layer conception**, which sees research as more of a process of uncovering layers to reach underlying meanings.

3   The **trading conception**, which sees research as about operating in a kind of 'social marketplace' and has a focus on products such as projects and publications.

4   The **journey conception**, which sees research very much as a personal, potentially transformational journey for the researcher.

If Brew is right there are some distinctly different ways of viewing research that may have a bearing on how we might introduce the idea of RDM.

The domino conception seems to be a rather process-orientated way of looking at research. We follow a set of procedures to produce a research outcome. RDM can fit this conception when we think about relating data management processes to the different steps in the research cycle. Actually, this is probably quite similar to how professional service staff might think of workflows that they want to link RDM to.

The trading conception seems to focus on products like publications or data. Again this can link to the RDM agenda through the value in the research 'marketplace' of objects like outputs and data. It should be easy to talk about RDM to people who think in terms of the trading conception, because they already think in terms of the value of certain objects.

The layer conception gives emphasis to the iterative nature of research in gradually uncovering layers of meaning. Perhaps the most interesting and challenging conception is that of the transformational journey. Here research is an immensely personal experience of discovery. It is a conception that reflects the profound uncertainty that challenging previous assumptions seems to imply. It is harder to see how RDM with its focus on processes and outputs can be aligned with this conception. Talking to researchers with this concept of research must respect the personal meaning they invest in 'data'.

Exploring further

We have spent a lot of time in this chapter reflecting on the nature of research. The most fascinating thing about RDM is really this link to the intriguing world of different communities of researchers. Getting a feel for the culture of different groups will be a central challenge for anyone supporting RDM. In the next chapter we focus more specifically on the complex concept of data.

We have already encouraged you to start having interesting conversations with researchers. This is important to build an understanding of their experience and so introduce RDM in a way sensitive to the sensibilities of researchers.

But it is also worth thinking about one's own experience of research. While you may never have done cutting-edge, publishable research, you may well have research experiences which give you a sense of what doing research feels like. We have found that people commonly undervalue the experience they have themselves had, when it can be a resource for building empathy.

Write a few notes for yourself about previous experiences. They could refer to:

- writing an undergraduate or masters dissertation
- research as part of developing a new process at work
- continuing professional development work
- research to answer enquiries from service users.

This work may not have the kudos attached to academic research; it may only have been about developing an understanding new to you, not new to the world; nevertheless it gives a valuable insight into the thoughts and feelings that go with research.

Further reading

Christine Borgman (2015) is a key author for those wishing to have a deeper understanding of RDM. This book is a must-read for her overview of how different fields of scholarship view data and the issues around data.

Borgman, C. L. (2015) *Big Data, Little Data, No Data: Scholarship in the networked world*, MIT Press.

References

Becher, T. and Trowler, P. (2001) *Academic Tribes and Territories: Intellectual enquiry and the culture of disciplines*, McGraw-Hill Education (UK).

Borgman, C. L. (2015) *Big Data, Little Data, No Data: Scholarship in the networked world*, MIT Press.

Brew, A. (2001) Conceptions of Research: A phenomenographic study, *Studies in Higher Education*, **26** (3), 271–85.

Klein, J. T. (1996) *Crossing Boundaries: Knowledge, disciplinarities, and interdisciplinarities*, University of Virginia Press.

CHAPTER 3

What are research data?

Aims

The aim of this chapter is to explore what research data are. It will help you start to have productive conversations with researchers about their data.

Research data are important to (some) researchers

For many researchers in the sciences and social sciences research data are of central importance to their work. Planning the collection of appropriate data is a key part of research design. The term 'data creation' may often be a more accurate term than 'data collection' or 'data capture', which imply that data are something existing before the researcher intervenes to actively construct them. But the language in use varies between fields of study and not all research projects actively create data. Creating data may take up many hours of work, and can be one of the most exciting parts of the research process, where the researcher gets into the laboratory or out into the field in the hope of finding something new. Then, processing the data and analysing them are central to creating new knowledge.

Skill and innovation in eliciting and then analysing data is central to one's success as a researcher. The researcher's deep relationship to data is strongly linked to their methodological commitments about how they believe science builds knowledge. A common understanding of methods is a central aspect of their subject discipline. Thus they have a strong investment in research data and a concern with their quality.

Actually, in many fields there is a kudos attached to collecting data oneself. It could be seen as a rite of passage for the novice researcher in some subjects. When talking about their work researchers often talk about 'my data . . . my stuff'. This points to the strong relationship between research, research data and identity. The conversation about research data is a deep one. We have even heard researchers talk about their data as their 'life's work'. Material they are gathering is part of building a legacy. Imagine the researcher who has pursued their interests over multiple projects throughout a long research career. To them they have an intimate connection to the various datasets that they have accumulated and pored over for many hours. Often it can be this, as much as pragmatic concerns such as fear of being beaten to publication, that inhibits research data sharing.

Having said all this, for many researchers data are essentially a means to an end: they are the foundation for gaining understanding of a phenomenon and then for publishing one's results. It is the understanding and the publications that matter more than the actual data.

Furthermore, some researchers would deny collecting 'data' at all. This might be because they see the term data as implying quantitative material such as survey data, when they deal with qualitative material such as interviews and observations. Or it may be that in their field one simply does not refer to evidence as 'data'. Thus, historians typically differentiate primary sources (original documents such as archival material) and secondary sources (interpreting the phenomenon that is studied, usually published works). Their primary sources are their data. So do not always start the conversation by talking about 'data'. If you do you run the risk of alienating humanities scholars.

Furthermore, some researchers genuinely don't collect data, e.g. in a purely theoretical field such as philosophy, arguably there are no data.

Talking to a researcher about the data they collect and analyse is a key conversation to have if you are working in the RDM field. But one has to be careful to use the terminology that researchers in that particular field relate to.

Exploring further

Start reading some papers produced by the researchers in the institution you work for, if you work for one, or an institution where you are studying. What are the data sources they are using? For example, in a social science or science paper the methodology section should describe in a fair amount of detail what the data were and how they were handled and analysed. The paper should reflect a particular methodological position.

Have a look at some research methods books for the same field. These also give you a sense of the typical sorts of research going on in that area and the data types in use.

Talk to a researcher about their work. Make a conscious effort to listen out for the terms they use to describe the research process and to categorise data. It may well be hard to understand the exact meaning of some of the measurements they make, if one does not have a related background. But one can begin to explore the issues that the researcher has about data quality.

Types of research data

Institutional surveys for RDM (see Chapter 9) often ask questions about research data such as how much data individuals have in gigabytes and what sort of data it is, e.g. whether it is in Word files, images, spreadsheets and so on.

Even if it is important to them and even if they do have lots of data, one should probably not rely too much on researchers' own estimates of the quantity of data they hold, or even the order of magnitude of data they have. Do you know how many megabytes of files you have on your work computer? Probably not; because there is no real need to know. When we ran an RDM survey at Sheffield in 2014 around a quarter answered 'don't know'. Many more who did answer may simply have been guessing.

Defining data by format, as in Table 3.1, may be useful for data management purposes, but it tells us little about what is in the document or spreadsheets.

Table 3.1 *Some formats of data*

Documents (Text, PDF, Microsoft Word)
Spreadsheets (for example: Microsoft Excel)
Websites
Notebooks/diaries
Databases (for example: Access, MySQL, Oracle)
Questionnaires, transcripts, codebooks
Audiotapes, videotapes
Film, photographs
Artefacts, slides, specimens, samples
Collection of digital objects acquired and generated during the process of research
Raw data files generated by software, sensors or instrument files
Models, algorithms, scripts
Contents of an application (input, output, log files for analysis software, simulation software, schemas)

Table 3.2 gives us an immediate sense of the range of types of data. Virtually anything could be data. It could be non-digital: it could be a material object or a completed printed questionnaire. If it is digital, it could be vast and complex; or small. Categories such as 'images' disguise the huge range of visual material used in research, from works of art and historical photos to satellite imagery and medical photography. One project might produce multiple forms of data.

Table 3.2 *Some types of data*

Results of experiments
Measurements collected in the field
Software programmes and their outputs
Interview audio recordings and transcripts
Focus group transcripts
Questionnaire responses
Government surveys
Images
Moving images
Historical documents
Physical objects
Social media data: tweets
Logs of web server traffic or another activity

From an RDM point of view this proliferation of data types is central to the challenge. For example, we may need to run a repository that handles at least part of this range of types of material. Inevitably the descriptive standards and documentation of data are also widely variable across subjects, and so similar types of data might be described in rather different ways.

Some definitions of research data

Read these definitions carefully, and consider their strengths and weaknesses:

Factual records (numerical scores, textual records, images and sounds) used as primary sources for scientific research, and that are commonly accepted in the scientific community as necessary to validate research findings. A research dataset constitutes a systematic, partial representation of the subject being investigated.   (OECD, 2007, 14)

Data are facts, observations or experiences on which an argument or theory is constructed or tested. Data may be numerical, descriptive, aural or visual. Data may be raw, abstracted or analysed, experimental or observational. Data include but are not limited to: laboratory notebooks; field notebooks; primary research data (including research data in hardcopy or in computer readable form); questionnaires; audiotapes; videotapes; models; photographs; films; test responses. Research collections may include slides; artefacts; specimens; samples.   (University College London, 2013)

Qualitative or quantitative statements or numbers that are (or assumed to be) factual. Data may be raw or primary data (e.g. direct from measure-ment), or derivative of primary data, but are not yet the product of analysis or interpretation other than calculation.   (Royal Society, 2012, 12)

Research data are defined as recorded factual material commonly retained by and accepted in the scientific community as necessary to validate research findings; although the majority of such data is created in digital format, all research data are included irrespective of the format in which it is created.
                                                                    (EPSRC, n.d.)

The data, records, files or other evidence, irrespective of their content or form (e.g. in print, digital, physical or other forms), that comprise a research project's observations, findings or outcomes, including primary materials and analysed data.   (Monash University, 2010)

Research data are the evidence that underpins the answer to the research question, and can be used to validate findings regardless of its form (e.g. print, digital, or physical). These might be quantitative information or qualitative statements collected by researchers in the course of their work by experimentation, observation, modelling, interview or other methods, or information derived from existing evidence. Data may be raw or primary (e.g. direct from measurement or collection) or derived from primary data for subsequent analysis or interpretation (e.g. cleaned up or as an extract from a larger dataset), or derived from existing sources where the rights may be held by others. Data may be defined as 'relational' or 'functional' components of research, thus signalling that their identification and value lies in whether and how researchers use them as evidence for claims. They may include, for example, statistics, collections of digital images, sound recordings, transcripts of interviews, survey data and fieldwork observations with appropriate annotations, an interpretation, an artwork, archives, found objects, published texts or a manuscript. The primary purpose of research data is to provide the information necessary to support or validate a research project's observations, findings or outputs.   (Concordat on Open Research Data, 2016)

The output from any systematic investigation involving a process of observation, experiment or the testing of a hypothesis, which when assembled in context and interpreted expertly will produce new knowledge.
(Pryor, 2012, 3)

Anything you perform analysis on.   (Briney, 2015, 6)

There are many definitions of data. In policy documents it may be useful to try and define research data in a fairly formal way, but some definitions seem to work much better for certain disciplines or meta-disciplines than others. For example, the Royal Society and EPSRC definitions apply more for science subjects. The UCL definition is useful for making it clear to all sorts of researchers that that 'stuff' they are creating is indeed data. It is more of a definition through listing examples than by focusing on what 'data' is conceptually. Briney's (2015) definition has the value of being simple and direct. The Monash definition perhaps confounds data and the findings based on that data. Pryor's definition focuses on the systematic process and the purpose, creating new knowledge, though the range of methods feels a little narrow. The most comprehensive definition is from the Concordat. The start of the Concordat definition focuses on purpose. The purpose of research data is to provide an answer to research questions. The Concordat also usefully differentiates various states of data e.g. raw, primary, derived data.

Exploring further

Collect some more definitions of research data and analyse them. Look at relevant national or international policy statements and see how they seek to define data. If your institution has a research data policy, how is data defined there? From your conversations with researchers which is the most useful definition?

Data collections

Individual scholars or projects may produce data collections: coherent bodies of data that others might want to re-use.

Thinking about collections of research data might be a rather 'library' way of looking at data, as if it's a coherent body of material with clearly defined scope. This might not be quite how a researcher would see their 'stuff'. They are probably more likely not to have really thought of it as a coherent body of material, just something they use and that grew organically. Nevertheless it can be a useful perspective for thinking systematically about the scope and content of a body of research data.

Carlson has advocated a structured interview for capturing a profile of a research dataset (http://datacurationprofiles.org). The data curation profile technique constitutes a rather comprehensive and systematic approach to finding out all about the data produced in a project or series of projects. The structure is itself a very useful way of thinking about the different aspects of data, even if it is actually something smaller or less tidy than a 'collection'. Some of the headings include:

- overview of the research, including the topic and funding source
- data kinds and stages – in the form of a narrative about the data collection, and including a data table itemising data collected by size, format and number of objects
- intellectual property rights relating to the data
- organisation and description of the data – including metadata standards in use
- target repository
- sharing and access – who can use the data and on what basis, including any desire for an embargo
- discovery – including target audiences
- tools – tools used in the research that others may need to use to re-use the data
- measures of impact – what usage measures would be appropriate to this material
- data management – practical issues, including back-up and security
- preservation – which material should be preserved and for how long.

If you are thinking of talking to a researcher about their data this approach gives you a systematic way of thinking.

Exploring further

Read some of the data curation profiles http://datacurationprofiles.org/.

Try and relate the proposed structure and some of your early conversations with researchers. Some questions may not feel relevant to a particular area of research. Work on a set of questions you feel comfortable asking a researcher.

Look at some datasets in the local data repository, a subject data repository or a general one like Dryad or Figshare and examine some of the deposits and how they have been described.

Data lifecycles

As well as data being created within the research lifecycle, data could be considered to have their own lifecycle. Data tend to go through a process of creation, cleaning, combination, storage, analysis, and possibly then preservation, sharing and re-use.

The metaphor of a lifecycle, be that of life to death or life to rebirth, has a strong resonance in the world of RDM. It has always been central to archival and preservation work. For example, the UK Data Archive (www.ukdataservice.ac.uk/manage-data/lifecycle) proposes a simple model with six stages:

- Creating data – this stage involves such activities as planning data collection, locating existing data sources and the actual data collection tasks, including documenting the data. In research involving human subjects it is highly likely to include the important ethics clearance stage.
- Processing data – validating and cleaning data, prior to the serious business of analysis.
- Analysing data – this the stage at which data are analysed and includes publication.
- Preserving data – this is about getting them into the right format for preservation and documenting them.
- Giving access to data – this includes making data discoverable, setting up conditions of re-use and promoting such re-use.
- Re-using data – including follow-up research and others re-analysing the data.

These are more like logical steps than the ones we might observe in any actual project. By definition such lifecycles are a simplification of real life, which is far less linear and more iterative in practice. Some commentators talk about research workflows rather than lifecycles: but this may make the complex and contingent patterns of research sound a bit too much like a defined administrative flow of work. Having said that, looking for temporal patterns is likely to be rewarding. Also, this is a data perspective on research. Most researchers would be more preoccupied with gaining grants, outputs and publication, than the life of the data. Again, this realisation needs to be borne in mind when trying to use the model.

Another rather famous representation of research data is the DCC curation model. Again, this is more like the data curator's vision of the lifecycle of data, than something a researcher would relate to strongly.

Exploring further

If you can, ask a researcher about the detailed steps in their research process. This will help you get to grips with the life of data. You might want to take the approach used by Mattern et al. (2015), who asked researchers to produce a hand-drawn diagram of the research process, and then asked them to add to the picture notes about actions relating to data. It might be best to focus on a particular research project, because there may be differences across different projects. Capturing more about the flow of the research process can help you map out where support is needed or can be offered within the research process. Comparing diagrams produced by researchers in the same field will give you a fascinating insight into the commonality and variation within a single research area.

Mattern, E., Jeng, W., He, D., Lyon, L. and Brenner, A. (2015) Using Participatory Design and Visual Narrative Inquiry to Investigate Researchers' Data Challenges and Recommendations for Library Research Data Services, *Program*, **49** (4), 408–23, http://doi.org/10.1108/PROG-01-2015-0012.

Research data is complex

There have already been some hints that research data is not simple; this section further explores the complexity of research data.

Commentators often refer to the five Vs of big data:

1 Volume
2 Variety
3 Velocity
4 Veracity
5 Value.

These aspects can serve as headings for thinking about research data, too. We have already discussed that researchers may not have a precise idea of the *volume* of data they have collected. Much of the early discussion of RDM was linked to the concept of a 'data deluge', vast quantities of data being created in big science and challenging to store and document for re-use. Researchers working in astronomy, for example, might well be involved in work generating truly vast quantities of data. Not all research does have great volume, though. The title of Christine Borgman's (2015) book *Big Data, Little Data, No Data* neatly captures the fact that not all research data has huge 'volume'. But just because the amounts concerned are not vast does not mean that they are easy to manage.

We have also already discussed the *variety* of data. This applies within individual projects as well as between disciplines. In their study of data in the life sciences, Williams and Pryor (2009) mapped researchers using a complex array of data sources and different tools. A single study may draw in multiple forms of data that have to be managed collectively. Some are actively created for the project, other data are background or reference data that does not necessarily get cited. Each sub-field they studied was very different.

By *velocity*, commentators on big data are referring to the continuously updated streams of data that might be produced by such sources as sensors or internet traffic. Of course, this very same material could well become research data. Not all researchers will be trying to handle such dynamic data, but it is useful to think about most research data as dynamic. Data should not be seen as a thing, like a specific spreadsheet. Data are multiple and changeable. Thus, a researcher might gather some measurements in the field. Then they would enter this raw data into a spreadsheet back in the office. After some quality checking there might be a new version (derived data). Manipulating the data might lead to new versions. Combining this with other data would produce further versions. Tangible examples of such processes are described in the next chapter. But the key conclusion is that data changes. This lies behind Borgman's (2015) question: 'When is data?' Something plays a role of being data at a particular moment.

To take another example, a researcher might conduct interviews, making audio recordings of them, and taking down some field notes to be associated with each one. They might well then transcribe the interview. Transcripts can be imported into some qualitative data analysis software for coding. Later one might tidy up an anonymised version of the interview transcript for sharing. Thus there are likely to be multiple versions of each interview, not necessarily a single definitive one. This creates data management (such as file naming) issues.

Such patterns of change are suggested by the lifecycle model. Yet processes of creation may be far more contingent, iterative and non-linear than a lifecycle model implies. Research is often akin to a craft skill. It is often not based on formulaic following of a closely defined recipe.

Data are also mobile across contexts. Some of the fascinating research on data journeys explores how data change meaning across different domains (Bates, Lin and Goodale, 2016). For example, weather station measurements (temperature, rainfall, etc.) are created by local, often volunteer, work in the spirit of creating open data. Combined with other similar weather measurements a weather dataset becomes a valuable commercialised source for the weather forecasters. It may also turn up as a valuable asset in the futures market on the stock exchange. Thus the meaning and value attached to data can alter as it moves between contexts.

Veracity is about the reliability of data. For the researcher the reliability of their data, data quality, is always a key issue. This could be about calibrating instruments or checking for outliers in a dataset. For a linguist it could be about precisely transcribing pauses in the transcription of a conversation. So what defines quality will be different, but it will always be a concern for researchers.

Again, research data vary in terms of their *value*. Some data are irreplaceable. They're the measurement of a unique event. They cannot be recreated. In other cases the cost would prohibit collecting them again. On the other hand, data produced from a computer model or simulation (e.g. in engineering or economics) can easily be reproduced. It is the model that needs to be preserved.

It is also worth reminding ourselves that digital data are fragile. They lose meaning out of the context of their collection if not documented. A spreadsheet without a key to the headings is more or less useless. The archival concept of provenance captures the importance of knowing about how an information object was created. A researcher wanting to re-use data will want to understand critical features of how the data were generated to be sure they can use them with confidence. What those critical features are, however, may vary.

Exploring further
Read the RIN report on life sciences (Williams and Pryor, 2009).

Continue to talk to researchers about their work. Try and understand more about the whole process of data creation and analysis – in the wider context of the research lifecycle. A visual analysis like the ones in the RIN report could be useful in mapping out how data is assembled and used. You might also think in terms of drawing up your own lifecycle model to capture the dynamic changes in the research life course.

Williams, R. and Pryor, G. (2009) *Patterns of Information Use and Exchange: Case studies of researchers in the life sciences*, Report by the Research Information Network and the British Library, www.dcc.ac.uk/projects/life-science-case-studies.

Information management and RDM

These complex aspects of research data help us start to grasp the importance of the information management aspects of RDM.

- Sometimes the researcher is battling to find storage for the sheer volume of 'active' data they are working on right now. They may also be forced to make choices about which data are preserved, because they have so much.
- Researchers need to manage different types of data in a coherent way over the lifetime of the project.
- Researchers are having to manage a flow of data sources which are themselves changing and malleable. When we talk about data re-use we are thinking about a complex contextual transition that is challenging to manage.
- Data quality is key to the reliability of the outcome of the research, and so its credibility. But what is critical to quality will vary.
- Data has central value to much (though not all) research. Empirical research turns on the interpretation of data. It takes up the researcher's time to produce. It may also literally cost money to license or have potential monetary value.

Research does have a strong information management component.

Further reading

Carol Tenopir's series of studies about scientists' views on research data are a key reference point for the field.

Tenopir, C., Allard, S., Douglass, K., Aydinoglu, A. U., Wu, L., Read, E., Manoff, M. and Frame, M. (2011) Data Sharing by Scientists: Practices and perceptions, *PLOS ONE*, **6** (6), https://doi.org/10.1371/journal.pone.0021101.

Tenopir, C., Dalton, E. D., Allard, S., Frame, M., Pjesivac, I., Birch, B., Pollock, D. and Dorsett, K. (2015) Changes in Data Sharing and Data Re-use Practices and Perceptions Among Scientists Worldwide, *PLOS ONE*, **10** (8), https://doi.org/10.1371/journal.pone.0134826.

If you want to read more look for the latest years' citations of these works.

At a more conceptual level Shankar's (2007) paper describes the element of judgement and convention that go into turning scientific work into something labelled data. Recognising the element of judgement and choice in this process helps us understand the way that any data is a construction in a particular context, rather than an objective object.

Shankar, K. (2007) Order from Chaos: The poetics and pragmatics of scientific recordkeeping, *Journal of the Association for Information Science and Technology*, **58** (10), 1457–66.

References

Bates, J., Lin, Y.-W. and Goodale, P. (2016) Data Journeys: Capturing the socio-material constitution of data objects and flows, *Big Data & Society*, **3** (2), http://doi.org/10.1177/2053951716654502.

Borgman, C. L. (2015) *Big Data, Little Data, No Data: Scholarship in the networked world*, MIT Press.

Briney, K. (2015) *Data Management for Researchers: Organize, maintain and share your data for research success*, Pelagic Publishing.

Concordat on Open Research Data (2016) www.rcuk.ac.uk/documents/documents/concordatonopenresearchdata-pdf.

EPSRC (n.d.) EPSRC Policy Framework on Research Data: Scope and benefits, www.epsrc.ac.uk/about/standards/researchdata/scope/.

Mattern, E., Jeng, W., He, D., Lyon, L. and Brenner, A. (2015) Using Participatory Design and Visual Narrative Inquiry to Investigate Researchers' Data Challenges and Recommendations for Library Research Data Services, *Program*, **49** (4), 408–23, http://doi.org/10.1108/PROG-01-2015-0012.

Monash University (2010) *Research Data Policy*, http://policy.monash.edu.au/policy-bank/academic/research/research-data-management-policy.html.

OECD (2007) OECD Principles and Guidelines for Access to Research Data from Public Funding, www.oecd.org/sti/sci-tech/oecdprinciplesand guidelinesforaccesstoresearchdatafrompublicfunding.htm.

Pryor, G. (ed.) (2012) *Managing Research Data*, Facet Publishing.

Royal Society (2012) *Science as an Open Enterprise*, https://royalsociety.org/topics-policy/projects/science-public-enterprise/report.

University College London (2013) *UCL Research Data Policy*, www.ucl.ac.uk/isd/services/research-it/documents/uclresearchdatapolicy.pdf.

Williams, R. and Pryor, G. (2009) *Patterns of Information Use and Exchange: Case studies of researchers in the life sciences*, Report by the Research Information Network and the British Library, www.dcc.ac.uk/projects/life-science-case-studies.

CHAPTER 4

Case study of RDM in an environmental engineering science project

Aims

The aim of the chapter is to give you a deeper insight into the nature of the issues around RDM by exploring a particular case study in some depth.

The project

In this chapter we will look at a case study of a particular research project. The focus is on the different types of data that are collected, created and reused. We will also use it to consider the challenges that the complexity of the research project present to the management of active data and their long-term preservation. The chapter gives you direct access to a researcher speaking about their work in their own words.

This case study consists of an interview with Steve Banwart, Professor of Environmental Engineering Science at the University of Sheffield. He is the leader of a large-scale project that is funded by the European Union. The project looks at how soil – one of our planet's essential natural resources – is produced and how it degrades. The aim is to quantify the impacts of environmental change on key functions of the soil and capture this in predictive models that can be used in decision making.

The project is international in scope. *Soil Transformations in European Catchments* (SoilTrec) brings together a network of over 30 research field sites. Professor Banwart explains that 'it has 16 different institutions, as partners located in 3 different continents.' The partner institutions are primarily in Europe, but also in the USA and in China.

Working with geographically dispersed teams that each collect data that need to be understood and ultimately combined with the data that other teams collect is quite a challenge in itself. But to add to the complexity of the project, these teams are also multidisciplinary and include, for example, engineers, chemists, biologists and physicists. It is therefore not surprising that the researchers working on the project handle a wide variety of data, sometimes in large quantities. This project handles data that are generated principally through observations and experiments in the field, 'digging holes in the ground and studying dirt, if you will', as well as laboratory experimentation. Data are also generated through computer modelling. And, Professor Banwart adds, 'we also use existing remote earth observation data, primarily satellite data and geographical information systems held by government agencies like the European Soil Bureau.'

The research method

So the research method is to study a property of soil called soil structure. And soil is made up of primary particles of small fragments of minerals from the parent rock that soil forms from, dead organic matter which is decaying (so you might think of plant remains which have been deposited on the soil, at the beginning of winter, and these are broken down by soil organisms) and then also living organisms in the soil (principally bacteria and fungi but also worms and so on). These constituents of soil, in fertile soil they tend to bind up together and form larger aggregates. So these principal fragments are quite small, they can be a thousandth of a millimetre in size. But in productive soils we find out that these particles stick together and it's not clear why these larger aggregates coincide with more productive, more fertile soils. So the first research challenge that we tackle is to understand how aggregate formation occurs and why it, for example, supports better nitrogen supply to plants, better phosphorus supply to plants, better potassium supply to plants, all important nutrients. It's to understand that and to be more quantitative in our understanding of that.

[We aim] to have measurements about these properties of soil, at these different field sites that I have discussed and then to put the understanding that we gain into mathematical models, computer models of how soil aggregation occurs, and how it is affected by environmental factors such as rainfall, temperature [and the] type of rock that the soil is on. Once these types of models are built then we apply these to decision making. For example we can think: 50 years from now, how much of the land around Sheffield will continue to be a national park with grassland, farmland perhaps to the east, grassland for farming to the north but then urban development all around the city? And so this type of modelling allows us to take a piece of land on the edge of Sheffield and say: how will this change? How will the soil conditions change if we change the land use? And then we can look forward 50 years in time through a prediction with our model. We can run it under a hypothetical scenario and see: this is what our mathematical model tells us will happen to soil over this period of time if we change the way we use the land. That allows us then to choose how we use the land, and so it gives a decision-making framework to help people formulate policy.

The data

It's a huge range of measurements. In the laboratory we use measurements from methods in chemistry, biology and physics. So in chemistry we might study the composition of the fragments of soil, the small particles that make up these larger aggregates. The same thing for the organic matter: what is the chemistry of the organic matter? What is its elemental composition? How much phosphorus is in it? How much nitrogen is in it? And then you go to microbiology, and we get data through genetic analysis of the organisms that are living in the soil, what types of organisms are there, what do they do? So a wide range of scientific data, that has to do with the details, are quite small-scale of what is happening in a grain of soil and in one of these soil aggregates.

And you can look at larger scale, the soil profile. So this might be a metre-length column of soil from the top of the land surface to the bottom of the soil layer. We might want to understand the flow of materials through this. So as rain falls on the surface, things that are dissolved in the rain, how do they move downwards with the water? The gases that are in the atmosphere, how do they move into the soil? Gases that are generated in the soil: for example, as bacteria decompose the organic matter, they generate carbon dioxide. That's a greenhouse gas. We might want to know how quickly that then moves back upwards out of the soil into the atmosphere. So we have measurements on all of these flows of materials through a column metre of scale.

Now let's move out of the lab into the field, and now we can think of a catchment. We can think of a stream flowing out of the Peak District near Sheffield. We can think of it draining into a reservoir for drinking water, and all that water as it's collecting in the upland regions and flowing downwards into the stream. Throughout that catchment we have soil and we want to think about this composition of the soil, and these flows of materials in and out of the soil, just as we studied in the lab. We have to think about this [on] the scale of the landscape across perhaps several kilometres in space, maybe 10 or 100 square kilometres. And so we need to make measurements there and so we might do that with aerial sensing, we might do that with some point measurements, like monitoring stream water flows at a specific place, measuring the composition of the water as it flows past that measuring point. We might want to have temperature sensors. We might want to have 5 or 10 or a million sensors distributed in the ground, telling us online with mobile phone technology back to a computer in the university how the soil moisture is changing over time at these different locations in the catchment.

So those are the types of measurements that we are getting in the field. Then you use that type of data to develop your computational models. Models generate a different type of data. This is synthetic data. We run the model and it generates fake measurements. We might measure the temperature, we might measure the amount of nitrate as a form of nitrogen dissolved in the water, but we would have a computational model that we run that will calculate through equations what would be the water flow, taking into account rainfall, and things like this, and what would be the nitrogen concentration taking into account how the bacteria in the soil are transforming nitrogen in different locations in the catchment. And so these models are generally spatially distributed. This means that we can have a calculation taking place at many points in this catchment. If it's a 10 square kilometre catchment we might want to have a calculation done on a square metre basis, so that's immediately 100,000, millions, 10s of millions of points that are being calculated and that would just be one time step. We might want to do this for 50 years, calculating this maybe not every second but maybe every day or if it's for a century maybe we want to calculate it on average for every month or every year. But you get the idea that these models can generate huge amounts of information. That adds another layer of data, in this case it's computationally generated data.

And many times to build these models, this is where we need these national data products. These could be Met Office data on climate, rainfall, temperature, air temperature, and so on. This could be from agencies such as the British Geological Survey and maybe their digital map of soils for the region. It could be from the Environment Agency and their database of river flows in the region. So there is a large amount of geographical data which we use in setting up these models and interpreting the results of the models and we need to draw on that as well.

Exploring further

Make a list of the type of data used in the project and then try and think through what risks each poses from an RDM perspective. Considering the different types of data and the way they are collected, what would be the main challenges for managing these data during the life of the project, and how would they be mitigated? You could, for example, think about the risks involved in inadequate data management and how these risks could be mitigated.

Building on this, what types of service could an institution create to support projects like this, do you think?

Steve Banwart explains what he thought were the main challenges and how he tackled them in the rest of the interview, so you can compare your own ideas with his.

The challenge of metadata

Professor Banwart states:

> The amount of data is probably less of a challenge in my area of research than the variety of the types of information you have to accommodate in digital format. A lot of it is just developing a culture within the project that people think about this, that people understand it's complicated, that they understand that in order to deliver the project you have to combine lots of different types of information, that all of us on the project have to know where the information is, what type of information there is, how it can be used. That's even before we start thinking about how we put it altogether in the model.
>
> So this notion of metadata, just general information that, you know, how do you build a card catalogue, how do you just decide to explain what is in your collection of information so that you can retrieve it easily, so that you can sort through it and come quickly to the pieces that you specifically need for certain applications? If you can just get your project team to recognise that needs to be done, and if you can do that well, that is a huge challenge. And that is an absolutely necessary step. And in my project we have been able to do it.
>
> And then it's another level of challenge to then actually be able to retrieve, judge the quality of the information, decide whether it's the right type of information, of the right quality to be useful. And then it's another step beyond that to actually start to put it together to draw scientific conclusions.
>
> So there are several layers that need to be dealt with, the first one is essential, without this recognition of the challenge, without having a culture of appreciating the challenge, understanding it and just tackling the first issue (which is how do you just categorise your information) it's a lost cause. It's impossible.

The need to foster a culture around metadata

From the very beginning of the project we set up a data management committee, led by a colleague on the project, with a strong personality, who is a good communicator and had a persuasive personal style and was not afraid to send lots of e-mails and ask for my help as the leader of the project to cajole, bully, bribe, plead with people. But from the very beginning we stated very clearly from my role as leader of the project that this was one of the number-one priorities in the project, that if we were going to deliver the project over the five years that it was going to run, we had to start with an attitude that data management was a priority and was going to be done well and that people had to, from the very beginning, start collecting the necessary information to provide this metadata.

And then we set up this data committee, we had enough project members throughout the project sitting on the data committee that we got some ownership of the problem distributed in the project and then we had a good leader handling that committee. A meeting on designing field investigations, and the laboratory investigations, where we also included the modelling teams. We all sat down together for an entire day and just made lists: this is what we have to measure, this is what we need to measure, this is the method that will be used to do it. We had to sit around a table, and bore each other silly with lists of data that was going to be obtained, how it was going to be obtained. Those lists were taken away by the people leading various parts of the project, and we just converted this into a more concise set of information that was better organised and this was implemented, in our case [in a] straightforward Microsoft Access database which is available to everybody on the project. It's on the Sheffield server, password-protected area, for any project partner to come in and look up where at least at one point in time everything was planned to be.

But then in addition to this, we also maintain a register of project results. This is just a Word document, just a table, that is updated by project partners. When a new set of results comes out of their lab or out of their computer models or out of their field site, they go on and register this, and it says what the data is, which bit of the metadata you can find the details, where you can find it, and just a note on how this is going to be used in the project. Then you can go to the metadata to get the details and then if you need to, you go to the individual scientists to retrieve let's say the values of the information, the actual numbers or whatever it is.

A lot of the data is maintained by the groups that made the measurements or ran the models and then in certain instances we have to combine these in a specific way, and then that becomes a dataset in its own right. These datasets, which are the combined datasets, which are often a combination of sets of different measurements, these go on the Sheffield server on a password-protected area and anyone in the project can go in and have a look at the data, they can actually retrieve the values.

Data sharing

Before the project started, as part of our project contract with the European Commission, we specified each of the deliverables which we anticipated and so on that list of results which are part of the contract we actually specified the degree of availability of the data: that it's solely within the consortium until it's released by the data management committee. [The committee is then] giving the green light, if you will. I don't think there is anything that we would have confidential in perpetuity. It is not so much about an issue of data that might be quasi-commercially confidential, like our competitors may use it to draw conclusions before we do. It's much more that in the scientific community, because of the peer review and general ethos of open sharing of data in publicly funded research, you want to make sure that what is out there, and that you are responsible for, is correct, is good. So it's much more about having a period of time of confidentiality to ensure the correctness of the data. And then there is always the issue of giving the people who generated the data the time to publish their academic journal results, because they feel some ownership. You have to respect that.

Exploring further

Make some structured notes around the main strategies Professor Banwart identifies for managing data within the project. Reflect again on what type of services the institution could put in place to deal with these kind of challenges. We will discuss different forms of institutional level research data service in Chapter 7.

What different forms of data sharing are apparent in this project and what were the main drivers? We will return to this question, at an abstract level, in the next chapter and again in Chapter 14 on Advocacy.

Talking to researchers

Listening closely to what researchers say about research data in their own words is a key activity in RDM. It is for this reason we have reproduced the interview at length. Although you probably know nothing about soil science it should be clear enough what kind of issues Professor Banwart faces in the project. He is particularly eloquent and clear in his explanation of the issues. But hopefully it has given you confidence that you can talk to researchers about their work from a research data perspective even if, inevitably, you do not understand the technicalities.

Perhaps we are surprised to find that managing data is central to the management of the whole project. Professor Banwart happily uses quite

Exploring further

Perhaps you would like to interview a researcher at your own institution to talk about the data in one of their research projects and what they think their research data management challenges were. You may find that smaller-scale projects have very different challenges from those found in SoilTrec. You could use some of the sources for interview questions discussed in Chapters 2 and 3.

technical terms like metadata, and even sees agreement about data management as a critical success factor for the project.

Further reading

If you want to read more about Professor Banwart's work see: Banwart, S. (2011) Save Our Soils, *Nature*, **474**, 151–2, doi:10.1038/474151a.
If you would like to read more case study material with researchers in different fields see:

RDMRose Learning Materials,
http://rdmrose.group.shef.ac.uk/?page_id=10#session-71-case-studies-of-researchers-and-research-projects.

CHAPTER 5

RDM: drivers and barriers

Aims

The aim of this chapter is to explore the forces that have led to RDM becoming important now, but also to explore why this has not led to change smoothly across every institution and for every researcher. It will prompt you to start to think about how these forces play out across particular institutions, such as one that you work for now or want to work for.

Introduction

This century has seen a gathering momentum behind the idea of research data management and open data.

Data sharing in the sciences has been common practice for many years. It is well established in such fields as meteorology, astronomy and genomics, for example. Data archives for particular fields of research have existed for half a century in many countries. For example, in the UK there has been a repository for social science-related datasets for decades, funded by the main government funder of social science research. Therefore there have also been for a while policies that mandate the deposit of material. Yet the extension of these ideas across the gamut of research is relatively new. Unravelling exactly how this has happened would probably take a book in itself, but it is instructive to explore some of the forces at work, because they pull in somewhat different directions and are still working themselves through. Some are pragmatic, some are ideological. How these arguments play out today at an institutional level will reflect the complexity of the underlying forces. Having a handle on these drivers is essential to positioning your own work effectively, in what is inevitably a rather politicised landscape.

To summarise what follows, much of the increasing stress on RDM can be traced back to the impact of digital technologies on how science is done, and particularly on the amount of data being generated in research and the potential to share it, because of the easy mobility of digital data. In addition, in some subjects there has also been a 'crisis of reproducibility': a loss of confidence in the integrity of scientific practice, resulting in a call for greater transparency. There is also a somewhat broader movement to reform research practice, often under the umbrella term 'open science'. Recognition of this by governments has been followed by research funders beginning to mandate data sharing. A number of international and national agencies have engaged heavily in building a socio-technical infrastructure in response. But much of the effort is being placed on researchers themselves and on the institutions they belong to, most notably universities. The following sections examine these trends in a bit more detail.

E-research

Most literature on policy development locates the key driver for the emergence of RDM policy in changes in the nature of science closely linked to digital technologies. In the late 1990s and at the beginning of the current century there was the emergence of a new wave of 'big science' founded on digital technologies, variously labelled 'cyberscience' or 'e-science', or 'e-research', in recognition of similar phenomena outside science, technical, engineering and medical (STEM) fields. Jankowski (2009, 7) identifies the main features of such new forms of research:

- increasing computerisation of the research process, often involving high-speed, large-capacity machines configured in a networked environment
- reliance on network-based virtual organisational structures for conducting research increasingly involving distant collaboration among researchers, often international in scope
- development of internet-based tools facilitating many phases of the research process, including communication, research management, data collection and analysis, and publication
- experimentation with new forms of data visualisation, such as social network and hyperlink analysis, and multimedia and dynamic representations
- publication, distribution and preservation of scholarship via the internet, utilising traditional and formal avenues (e.g., publishing houses, digital

libraries) as well as those less formal and less institutionalised (e.g., social networking sites, personal websites).

Thus, big science projects implied changes to the research process, how data is analysed, new patterns of collaboration, and new ways of disseminating results. In particular, very large amounts of data are being produced in some big science, in fields such as astronomy, bioscience, environmental science, particle physics, medicine and some social sciences. Some classic examples are the Digital Sky Survey, which was alleged to have created more data in its first week than had been created in the whole history of previous astronomy. The internet itself generates vast quantities of data that are being used for research purposes, e.g. Twitter streams.

The implications were influentially recognised in Hey and Trefethen's (2003) paper 'The Data Deluge: an e-science perspective'. The paper anticipated a flood of data being created by e-science projects and the need for an infrastructure to support their management and preservation: digital curation. More positively, digital technologies also offer the cheap storage and easy sharing of data, making the notion of open data a viable one. Increasing recognition of these changes was a trigger for an increasing interest in digital data curation.

We think it would be a little simplistic to locate such changes simply in technology drivers. Underlying the focus on large-scale, big-science projects was probably an intensification of the way that governments were using science to promote desired ends, particularly economic growth, and to solve complex social problems. But starting here in big science, increasing recognition of the relevance of managing and sharing data in all subjects gradually spread.

The 'crisis of reproducibility'

A more specific issue has also had some part to play in driving the RDM agenda, at least in some specific disciplines: namely a crisis in confidence around the integrity of some work being done in the field, and a strong feeling of a need for greater transparency. Two disciplines in particular have seen crises around the issue of the reproduction of research findings. One of these fields is biomedicine. In 2011 scientists from a German pharmaceutical lab wrote a paper revealing that they had found it impossible to reproduce the results of most of 47 studies of drug targets that they had tried to replicate (Prinz et al., 2011). The next year, it was reported in *Nature* that 47 of 53 landmark studies in cancer research could also not be reproduced (Begley and Lee, 2012). The conclusion some commentators drew was that these problems were not just the result of error, caused by the increasing complexity of experiments, but arose from the pressure on researchers to come up with positive results for publication.

Psychology is another discipline that has experienced something of a crisis around reproduction of results. There have been some prominent cases of downright fraud. Marc Hauser (Harvard) and Diederik Stapel (Tilburg) simply made up data. Such cases are damaging enough to the image of the subject, but again may reflect a more deep-seated problem around the pressures put on researchers to produce exciting results. Thus, a survey of psychologists conducted by John, Loewenstein and Prelec (2012) found that many researchers admitted to what the authors consider 'questionable research practices'. A few respondents admitted downright falsification of data! But many others admitted to dubious practices in an effort to make results look more significant:

- 0.6% of respondents surveyed admitted to falsifying data
- 22% said they had rounded off p-values, e.g. saying they had got 0.05 when it was 0.054
- 45.8% said they had selectively reported what 'worked'
- 38.2% said that they decided whether to exclude data after looking at the effect of doing so.

These are critical issues because much scientific research seeks to build on the foundations of previous work. If classic research findings cannot be reproduced, the domino effect is to undercut all that follows. Such issues potentially undermine the credibility of the whole subject as a discipline.

These problems link into a more fundamental questioning of science by the public and by politicians in an age of scepticism about experts. There is increasing pressure on science to explain results to the public.

The idea that previous research should be reproduced is not found in all disciplines. It also does not necessarily imply open data sharing. However, it is an important part of the context of the research data management agenda, particularly in certain fields.

Open science

The arguments about RDM do not exist in a vacuum; rather, they are clearly linked to wider discussions about the future of science, understood in its broadest sense and so including humanities and social sciences. Open science is an umbrella term that touches on many of these.

> Open science commonly refers to efforts to make the output of publicly funded research more widely accessible in digital format to the scientific community, the business sector, or society more generally.
>
> (OECD, 2015, 9)

It links open access to research outputs and open research data, but also encompasses other aspects of openness during the research process.

As with many agendas (including RDM), there are multiple, somewhat divergent strands of thinking tied up with open science. Fecher and Friesike (2014) suggest there are five somewhat different discourses or 'schools' of open science. They are not to be seen as crudely distinct, overlapping in most actual cases, but do have a rather different emphasis in how they interpret the concept:

1 In the **infrastructural school** open science is conceived primarily as a technology challenge. It explores how tools that support open collaboration and sharing are built.
2 The **public school** itself has two aspects. Firstly there is the perceived need for scientists themselves to reach out and explain their work to the public. So it is about the public communication of science. A second aspect is to involve the public directly in the scientific process itself, e.g. through collecting or even analysing data. The Galaxy Zoo project is a well known example of a project where the public can contribute by classifying astronomical data. Thus it is about the value of citizen science. It might also link to crowdsourcing science.
3 The **measurement school** has a somewhat different emphasis. It is concerned with improving the way the influence and impact of research can be captured.
4 The **democratic school** is concerned with ensuring that everyone has access to the results of research, as an aspect of democratic right to knowledge, especially where it has been funded by public money in the first place. So whereas the public school is about creating

different ways for the public to be involved, and making science more accessible, the democratic school is primarily concerned with ensuring that the existing types of outputs are available to all.

5 Finally, the **pragmatic school** regards open science as improving the efficiency of science through the benefits of researchers working together more.

Exploring further

Think about whether open science is a useful reference point for an institution you are interested in. Because it uses the term 'science' it seems to have a STEM focus. Also the term 'open' is controversial, because it strongly links to open access for research outputs and other notions of openness. The case for openness may be different in different contexts. Fecher and Friesike (2014) offer an interesting analysis that does tease out different strands of thinking that are easily elided. See Chapter 14 on advocacy more specifically on the various types of case that can be made for RDM and how different audiences might react differently to different types of argument.

Government and funder policy

Some of the origins of the current changes in policy around data can be located to the turn of the century, when the OECD began to explore issues around research data. A *Declaration on Access to Research Data from Public Funding* was issued at a ministerial-level meeting in early 2004. This was further developed through consultation as *Principles and Guidelines for Access to Research Data from Public Funding* (OECD, 2007). OECD recommendations are not legally binding or precise guidelines, but represent a statement of political commitment by its 30 members that are expected to be carried through into action.

The preface to the guidelines locates the drivers for change in the principles of openness in public science and the potential of digital technologies. The aim of the guidelines is to 'promote a culture of openness and sharing of research data'. Accessibility of research data is said (OECD, 2007) to be important for:

- the good stewardship of the public investment in factual information
- the creation of strong value chains of innovation
- the enhancement of value from international co-operation.

More specifically, access to data is seen as beneficial because it:

- reinforces open scientific inquiry
- encourages diversity of analysis and opinion
- promotes new research
- makes possible the testing of new or alternative hypotheses and methods of analysis
- supports studies on data collection methods and measurement
- facilitates the education of new researchers
- enables the exploration of topics not envisioned by the initial investigators
- permits the creation of new datasets when data from multiple sources are combined.

There are thus a number of key arguments at work. The very first point, and subsequent text, emphasises the importance of careful management of data that has been created at vast public expense. Thus the underlying argument is in terms of public investment. The following points seem to emphasise the value of data sharing to stimulating collaboration in research. By talking about 'diversity of analysis and opinion' there seems to be a link to basic democratic values. Other points tend to focus on the more immediate benefit to improved science, e.g. by enabling data to be re-used in ways the original collector had not imagined, to enable new research by combining datasets or doing meta-analyses on methods, and training new researchers.

The document then sets out and explains 13 principles that should govern the policy:

1 openness
2 flexibility
3 transparency
4 legal conformity
5 protection of intellectual property
6 formal responsibility
7 professionalism
8 interoperability
9 quality
10 security

11 efficiency
12 accountability
13 sustainability.

To pick out a few key points here. Starting with 'openness' gives emphasis to this as the ultimate ideal. It implies easy access at the lowest possible cost. Legal conformity recognises a number of specific restrictions on what can be shared, e.g. to protect privacy and confidentiality of human subjects and national security. Flexibility, interoperability and sustainability seek to define conditions for an effective infrastructure, in a rapidly changing technical environment.

Exploring further
Download this foundational document. Examine the explanations of the 13 principles. From your current knowledge, which seem to be the most significant or most surprising?

Policy developments

Over the decade since the *Guidelines*, more detailed policies, plans and investment in the OECD member states (and beyond) have gradually begun to emerge. This has not been a smooth or uniform process. In the UK we note an early wave of activity by government funding agencies, linked to the *Guidelines*. The economic crisis and a change of government led to a strengthening of requirements in the period 2008–12. A key year internationally seems to have been 2013, when a number of major government bodies made a commitment around RDM:

- White House Memorandum, 26 February
- Global Research Council Action Plan, 30 May
- G8 Science Ministers Joint Statement, 12 June
- European Union Parliament, 13 June.

In a book like this we cannot trace in detail developments in every country. Different countries have followed somewhat different paths, e.g. the experience in Australia led by ANDS and the USA are compared by Treloar, Choudhury and Michener (2012). Taken as a whole, a number of shifts of focus can be identified, e.g. away from an emphasis on digital curation and preservation issues with data, toward research data management, i.e. managing research data throughout the process of research.

What we can say here is that there has been a move internationally towards the ideal of sharing data, and increasingly the funders of research mandate this. That means that researchers are expected by default to share the data openly at the end of their project, as a condition of their funding. It is in this context that institutional-based research data services have emerged to help researchers do this, because on the whole governments have placed the onus on research organisations to create a support infrastructure, rather than funding centralised national services.

In the UK, for example, a large number of funders, both governmental and charities, have come together to align their requirements around the *Concordat on Open Research Data* (2016). Its ten principles are:

1 Open access to research data is an enabler of high-quality research, a facilitator of innovation and safeguards good research practice.
2 There are sound reasons why the openness of research data may need to be restricted but any restrictions must be justified and justifiable.
3 Open access to research data carries a significant cost, which should be respected by all parties.
4 The right of the creators of research data to reasonable first use is recognised.
5 Use of others' data should always conform to the legal, ethical and regulatory frameworks, including appropriate acknowledgement.
6 Good data management is fundamental to all stages of the research process and should be established at the outset.
7 Data curation is vital to make data useful for others and for long-term preservation of data.
8 Data supporting publications should be accessible by the publication date and should be in citable form.
9 Support for the development of appropriate data skills is recognised as a responsibility for all stakeholders.
10 Regular reviews of progress towards open access to research data should be undertaken.

The *Concordat* can be seen as a mature policy response to the challenges around RDM. The opening principle asserts the value of open access to data, as enabling better research and ensuring transparency and integrity. The second principle recognises the potential limits on the possibility of open data, but tries to place the emphasis on the researcher justifying any restrictions. The cost of sharing material is also acknowledged in point 3 and point 9 brings out the importance of giving researchers the right skills as a condition for it being possible. Point 4 reflects a researcher concern that having put the effort into collecting data they should have time to make first use of it. The last point brings out the need to review progress towards the goal of open access.

Journal policies

In line with the shift of policy, it is also significant to note that journals are increasingly also mandating sharing data related to publication. This adds a further driver for authors to consider RDM. They may well have to share data and details of analysis in order to get their work published. Journal policies involve not just sharing the data, but also providing documentation e.g. on code books as well as code used in analysis. This also implies reviewers checking the working.

The Transparency and Openness Promotion (TOP) guidelines (https://cos.io/our-services/top-guidelines) help define more precisely eight different types of requirement for reproducibility, and increase standardisation across different journals. It recognises disciplinary difference by setting three levels for each standard.

FAIR data principles

Another important set of principles that seems to be gaining wide support are the four FAIR guiding principles for data. These are high-level, technology/solution-neutral statements of the requirements for an effective data infrastructure:

- **Findable** – both people and machines should be able to find and re-find data. This implies persistent and unique identifiers for data, such as digital object identifiers (DOIs). It also implies suitable descriptive metadata to allow the data to be found. It further implies keeping the data in a visible catalogue or repository.
- **Accessible** – both people and machines should be able to access data through well defined, open protocols.

- **Interoperable** – implies that both the data and metadata describing it follow standards.
- **Re-usable** – implying that the data is fully documented, in terms of its provenance (e.g. who created it under what conditions) and that usage conditions are defined.

Data citation

A key aspect of promoting a culture of data sharing is a universally recognised way to cite data. Citation of data is also the basis for measuring its impact and rewarding the creator. The Data Citation Synthesis Group (Martone, 2014) have produced a widely referenced set of principles for data citation – the actual layout of a citation will vary depending on which referencing system (APA, Chicago, Harvard, etc.) is used. The eight principles are:

1 **Importance** – data are a significant output of research and therefore should be cited in the same way as papers and books.
2 **Credit and attribution** – it is important that the originators of a dataset should be given credit.
3 **Evidence** – where a claim is made relying upon data, that data should be cited.
4 **Unique identification** – data should have a unique identifier, just like an ISBN for a book.
5 **Access** – any citation should enable the person (or computer) to have a means to access the actual data.
6 **Persistence** – the identifiers need to continue to exist into the future.
7 **Specificity and verifiability** – identifiers should be granular enough to identify the actual data which supports the claim.
8 **Interoperability and flexibility** – citation should support differences in use across communities but also be common, so that interoperability is possible.

Digital Object Identifiers, the same unique identifiers as for journal articles, have emerged as the main way to give data a unique ID.

Exploring further

Do some desk research tracking down the foundational statements by your own government and its public funding agencies. It is worth reading these documents quite closely and trying to tease out which kinds of argument for research data management are given emphasis. Comparing documents you have found to the OECD *Principles* and the *Concordat* will help you do this.

RDM and the 'new public management'

In many respects funders mandating the careful management and sharing of data is a positive development for the creation of institutional research data services (RDS). Indeed, the emergence of such services can be closely linked to the impetus provided by such top-down directives. Nevertheless, by themselves funder mandates do not ensure that researchers themselves embrace data sharing. Indeed, many of the mandates have not been followed up with checking of compliance or with funding for the infrastructure and training needed to carry them through. In this context institutions are still left with dilemmas about how much to invest in RDS.

More fundamentally, if we locate some of the drivers behind the agenda in increasing desire to control and shape research for political purposes, we can see how there might be some resistance to the whole agenda. Monitoring the results of public funding of research at some level is surely justified where public funds have been given to conduct research. But for some commentators this can be seen as part of a wider trend towards the loss of academic autonomy, reflected in the increasing stress on measuring academics' performance through metrics like dollars of funding won or crude citation counts. The trends towards trying to manage a university as if it were a for-profit organisation is sometimes called the 'new public management' and is linked to the popular critique of 'neo-liberalisation'. For these commentators the value of universities exists in their being an independent and potentially critical voice in society. Not all research can be justified by its economic or immediate social benefits. In this context the RDM agenda could be construed as yet another form of government control and constraint over the independence of research.

Critically, if we focus on the policy arguments for RDM it also means that it can be a largely top-down agenda. This is probably not desirable. To be effective there needs to be a strong degree of commitment from research communities themselves to RDM because it is only they who can work out the meaning of open data. The argument from a funder mandate is ultimately quite limited; a stick rather than a carrot approach, that will not necessarily play out well and certainly not lead to a rich culture of data sharing. Or more simply, RDM has the potential, if not handled carefully, to appear just like another demand on the busy researcher 'getting in the way of doing the actual research' and spawning another layer of 'bureaucracy'. Positioning a research data service as a positive benefit, in the researcher's own interest, is critical to its success.

Drivers and barriers
Drivers
So far in this chapter we have reflected the growing strength of the movement for improved research data management. Some slightly different end-points are imagined. Many of the policy statements emphasise the value of sharing data, perhaps completely openly, though many would recognise the need for some restrictions. A narrower type of argument might revolve around the value of research data management, since it is obviously better for the researcher to manage their data efficiently, even if there is not an intention to share. Some of the key drivers can be summarised as:

- Big data, digital data: research increasingly produces large quantities of data. The researcher needs ways to store and access this data securely during the project. Their digital nature makes them much easier to store at low cost and also to share at fairly low cost. Digital data are also fragile.
- Openness might be seen as inherently good, be that for scientific transparency or for more political reasons.
- Reproducibility and research integrity more generally are enhanced through transparency. Making data available makes reproduction studies possible.
- New research is made possible through data sharing.
- Immediate benefits to researchers themselves arise from better data management in terms of avoiding data loss or time wasted.

It is easy to elide some of these arguments, but they can be separate and point in different directions. Not all these arguments apply to all areas of research. For example, some researchers are simply not producing massive amounts of data; in some fields research is rarely reproduced.

Barriers

Equally we have to acknowledge a range of challenges. Some of these could be:

- Multiple agendas – the very diversity of the arguments for RDM add to the complexity of advocacy.
- Institutional politics, limited funding and alternative priorities – what sort of priority should be given to RDM relative to the many other institutional priorities? What is the benefit/risk to the institution?
- Funder mandates may not be monitored or enforced, in which case it remains critical how far the institution regards being a good citizen as a priority.
- Designing a technical infrastructure that fits in with workflows of researchers.
- Commercial exceptions, where research is funded by a commercial partner who for competitive reasons wants the data and results to be kept secret.
- Legal or ethical exceptions, where there is a potential violation of personal rights if data is shared.
- Research cultures and general inertia – ultimately sharing data will not work if there are no practices of re-use.
- Methodological issues – more directly, sharing certain types of data to be re-used by someone who did not collect it is often seen as a deep problem.
- Researcher skills – do researchers have the skills to identify data that is worth preserving and documenting it in an accurate way so that it can be found and used?
- Bureaucracy.
- Academic freedom – arguments from the need for researchers to maintain their autonomy.

Exploring further

Figure 5.1 lays out some of the drivers and barriers in the form of a force field analysis diagram. Drivers are represented by arrows pointing to the right; barriers point in the opposite direction. In force field analysis you size the arrows to represent the strength of the driver or barrier. Do some work thinking about how strong you think these forces are for your institution. It may vary in different faculties. Where are the critical areas?

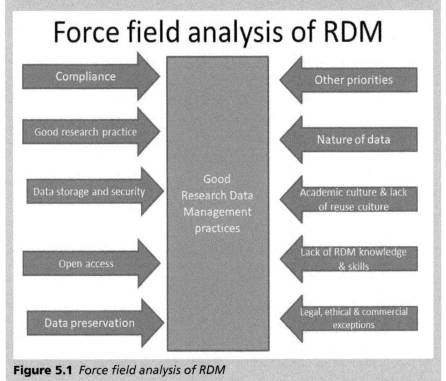

Figure 5.1 *Force field analysis of RDM*

Further reading

If you are interested in the question of what open science means to scientists, as well as Fecher and Friesike (2014) you could read the following paper:
Levin, N. and Leonelli, S. (2017) How Does One 'Open' Science? Questions of value in biological research, *Science, Technology & Human Values*, **42** (2), 280–305.

Analysis of the changing nature of e-research can be explored through:
Meyer, E. T. and Schroeder, R. (2015) *Knowledge Machines: Digital transformations of the sciences and humanities*, MIT Press.

References

Begley, C. G. and Lee M. E. (2012) Drug Development: Raise standards for preclinical cancer research, *Nature*, **483**, 531–3.

Concordat on Open Research Data (2016)
www.rcuk.ac.uk/documents/documents/concordatonopenresearchdata-pdf.

Fecher, B. and Friesike, S. (2014) Open Science: One term, five schools of
thought, in Bartling, S. and Friesike, S. (eds) *Opening Science: The evolving
guide on how the internet is changing research, collaboration and scholarly
publishing*, Springer International Publishing, 17–47.

Hey, A. J. G. and Trefethen, A. (2003) The Data Deluge: An e-science
perspective, in Berman, F., Fox, G. and Hey, A. J. G. (eds) *Grid
Computing: Making the global infrastructure a reality*, Wiley, 809–24.

Jankowski, N. W. (2009) The Contours and Challenges of E-research. In
Jankowski, N. W. (ed.) *E-Research: Transformation in scholarly practice*,
Routledge, 3–34.

John, L. K., Loewenstein, G. and Prelec, D. (2012) Measuring the Prevalence
of Questionable Research Practices with Incentives for Truth Telling,
Psychological Science, **23** (5), 524–32.

Martone, M. (ed.) (2014) Data Citation Synthesis Group: Joint Declaration of
Data Citation Principles San Diego CA: FORCE11,
www.force11.org/group/joint-declaration-data-citation-principles-final.

OECD (2007) OECD Principles and Guidelines for Access to Research Data
from Public Funding, www.oecd.org/sti/sci-tech/oecdprinciplesand
guidelinesforaccesstoresearchdatafrompublicfunding.htm.

OECD (2015) Making Open Science a Reality, *OECD Science, Technology and
Industry Policy Papers*, No. 25, OECD Publishing, Paris,
http://dx.doi.org/10.1787/5jrs2f963zs1-en.

Prinz, F., Schlange, T. and Asadullah, K. (2011) Believe it or not: How much
can we rely on published data on potential drug targets? *Nature Reviews
Drug Discovery*, **10**, 712.

Treloar, A., Choudhury, G. and Michener, W. (2012) Contrasting National
Research Data Strategies: Australia and the USA, in Pryor, G. (ed.)
Managing Research Data, Facet Publishing, 173–203.

CHAPTER 6

RDM as a wicked challenge

Aims

The aim of this chapter is to explore the nature of research data as a management and leadership issue, in particular in the light of the distinction between 'tame' and 'wicked' challenges.

Types of problem

Management in any context involves tackling problems. However, it may be useful to distinguish different types of problem, because they demand a slightly different managerial approach and skillset.

In everyday management there are plenty of 'tame' problems. These are known issues that we have well-trodden ways of dealing with. For example, we need to change our policy to respond to a new government initiative or law. We review the change, look at our existing procedures, talk to different stakeholders and try and devise a new policy. Then we publicise the change and offer training. After a while we evaluate how well the change has been put into practice. The management problem is simply to manage the resources available to carry through a fairly familiar set of steps.

At the other end of the spectrum of complexity and uncertainty are what are sometimes called 'wicked' problems or challenges. These are far less familiar and understood; they are so entangled with multiple issues it is hard to know even where to start to address them. We may not be quite sure what sort of outcome we really want. Perhaps there is no 'solution' to them, only ways of coping. It follows that the approach to management and leadership in this kind of context requires us to operate differently from addressing the tame problem.

> **Exploring further**
> We find this idea of different types of problem an immensely interesting
> one. Reflect on an area of professional or personal life and see if you can
> identify a tame and a more wicked type of issue. Recognising the difference,
> do you approach the issues differently?

The wicked challenge concept

The concept of a wicked problem was originally defined in urban planning
in the 1970s by Rittel and Webber (1973). An analogous concept is the
'social mess', a term coined by Horn and Weber (2007). Thinking about
applying the concept to RDM, Cox, Pinfield and Smith (2016) suggested
that we could synthesise such work to produce a list of features of a
wicked challenge. Adapting Cox et al.'s concepts slightly:

1   There is no definitive formulation of a wicked challenge. One of the
    problems of a wicked problem is that different stakeholders cannot
    agree on exactly what the question at issue really is. This reflects
    radically different perspectives on the same situation, itself arising
    from the way complex problems draw together stakeholders from
    different domains and social worlds.
2   There is a 'no stopping rule'. A wicked challenge is with us now. It is
    affecting us now, so we do not seem to have time to stop to take
    stock and think.
3   There is no test of whether a solution will work or has worked. We
    know when the tame problem has been solved, because we have a
    clear concept of the desired endpoint. With a complex problem we
    do not really know where we are.
4   Every solution is a 'one-shot operation'. There can be no gradual
    learning by trial and error, because each intervention changes the
    problem in an irreversible way.
5   There is no comprehensive list of possible solutions. Most
    management relies on a toolbox of techniques that are used over and
    over again, such as researching a problem, talking to people or
    looking at what has worked for others. With a wicked challenge we
    don't have that toolbox available.
6   Each wicked problem is unique, so that it is hard to learn from
    previous problems because they were different in significant ways.
    Often when we encounter a new issue the penny quickly drops that

this is like a previous problem and that what we learned before can be applied again, with a little adaptation. The wicked challenge is genuinely new. Our past learning may equip us poorly to deal with the new situation. We cannot turn to past models that we know will work.

7　A wicked problem is itself a symptom of other problems. Incremental solutions run the risk of not really addressing the underlying problem. It is the interconnectedness of the wicked challenge that makes it problematic. Settling one aspect of it only shows that there is a knock-on effect elsewhere that was not predicted.

8　There is a choice about how to see the problem, but how we see the problem determines which type of solution we will try to apply.

9　As well as there being no single definition of the problem, there are multiple value conflicts wrapped up in it. At the heart of the wicked challenge are incommensurable value conflicts. No approach will satisfy everyone, by definition. There is a profound lack of consensus.

10　There are also multiple ideological, political or economic constraints on possible solutions. Most of the issues we tackle on a daily basis can be solved within existing resources. The organisation's purpose is to remember and carry through these kinds of fixes. But the scale of a wicked challenge puts it beyond the resources available.

11　There is great resistance to change. As well as resources being scarce the inertia in the situation makes it hard to make progress.

12　With social messes, in addition to the complexity of the problem itself, data to describe the problem are often uncertain or missing. It may even be difficult to actually collect information – especially if the dimensions of the problem are unclear. There is also no one expert with the answer. With a tame problem we have systems in place to capture decision-making information in a timely way. We know what is going on. If we are stuck there is an expert who can parachute in and solve it. But the scale and complexity of the wicked challenge means we tend to lack the data on which to analyse the problem clearly. Also there is no kind of professional whose expertise offers a solution to every aspect of the challenge.

13　Because the problems are complex, there are multiple possible intervention points.

14　The consequences of any particular intervention are difficult to imagine.

If we are thinking of examples of wicked problems we may immediately think of complex and divisive political issues that are at the heart of long-running conflict. RDM is scarcely an issue at this level of complexity and challenge. Nevertheless, it may be useful to think about some of the ways that RDM really is 'wicked'. In an increasingly interconnected, globalised world more of our professional issues are coming to have this quality of scale, complexity and ambiguity.

Is RDM wicked?

There are some *prima facie* grounds for thinking RDM does have a significant degree of wickedness:

- National and international policies have become stronger, clearer and more consistent, it could be argued, but the underlying drivers are several and pull in slightly different directions: open access, pragmatic need, replicability.
- The scale and reach of the challenge is significant, for it implies a change to the research practices of every researcher in an institution.
- The diversity of research complicates the issues. There are a large number of disciplinary and sub-disciplinary research cultures among researchers, each with their own notion of what data are. Thus there is a lack of a common language or common practice.
- The complexity of the research process, and the fluid character of what data are, are also a problem with scoping the challenge in a clear way.
- The symbolic status of research within institutions means that change is fraught with issues of power and identity.
- There is a lack of consistent funding for RDS.
- The lack of clarity about which existing support services would be the natural lead for RDS muddies the waters around institutional service. Because it's a grey area between professional domains it throws up sharply contrasting interpretations.

When we talked to professional service staff about RDM in the light of the wicked challenge concept, they wrote some narratives of experiences that capture the wickedness of RDM.

In our institution a small group of individuals from [Computing], the library, senior management, research support and records management met several times to discuss RDM and each time we struggled with the concept of RDM. It was very difficult to agree on how and where to start to tackle the problem. Each meeting seemed to take one step forwards and half a step back!

1 Some researchers don't see themselves as producing data: so what's the problem?
2 Some researchers already 'look after' their data: so what's the problem?
3 Surely we just need to give researchers more storage: so what's the problem?
4 We have an RDM policy in place now: so what's the problem?

. . . consider the story of a typical academic, who has career aspirations (which are often judged via high quality research and publications) and no free time. When speaking to this academic about the research data that is produced, multiple issues arise immediately. These vary from not knowing what data is, where to deposit it, what to deposit, why to deposit it, how to link it with publications, what to do when data changes, and what is active data or archival data, etc. When speaking to them about Data Management Plans (DMP), they consider it the least important part of the funding bid process. Each of these issues then raise further questions which illustrate the wicked nature of RDM.

Creating DOIs for data is apparently simple. Pay your fee to DataCite, submit a bit of XML with at least the core metadata fields. Make sure you have a landing page. Job done.

These are some of the issues this 'simple' proposition has thrown up:

• What granularity should DOIs be created at? – which is in turn related to how you structure the data, which is in turn related to your philosophical approach to the data and how closely you want to link it with specific publications – or not.
• There is some overlap between [an institution's data repository] content and data centre content – what do we do if a dataset already has a DOI?
• What about data that is managed by the institution but not necessarily in a central repository? How can we be sure the landing pages will be maintained? What happens if the data moves and is hosted elsewhere?
• Researchers want to include DOIs in their publications; do we allocate DOIs before we have received the data or insist on a deposit prior to allocating the DOI?

Exploring further

Read the quotes and try and link them back to the characteristics of a wicked challenge as defined earlier in the chapter. Can you think of a story yourself that captures the wicked nature of RDM?

The first narrative illustrates the difficulty of getting a handle on the problem itself. We have a series of meetings, but we aren't getting nearer to delimiting the problem. This illustrates features of wicked challenges such as 1 and 8 in the list above.

The second narrative illustrates this further by revealing that many stakeholders, including senior managers, refuse to acknowledge that there is a problem at all. Within a narrow professional interpretation there is a solution, but from a broader perspective there is a problem. Getting RDM onto institutional agendas remains an issue.

The third narrative captures the point of view of the individual academic, for whom the problem is complex, hard to define and has to be addressed in the context of the pressure to solve many other problems.

The final narrative reveals the way that any technical solution actually raises many complex issues that themselves require significant effort to resolve.

Whether RDM is truly a wicked challenge is debatable. It can scarcely be compared to climate change, a classic wicked problem. But particularly as a new agenda it does have some wicked aspects: it cuts across multiple professional divides; we lack much information about the current state of affairs; it is subtly different from previous challenges we have faced; it appears as a complex new agenda at a time of resource restraint.

Leadership in a wicked challenge context

Of course, the whole point of differentiating a wicked challenge is to prompt us to approach it differently from a tame problem. It is not to be dealt with through familiar tried and tested methods; rather, we need to start to think differently.

Grint (2008) offers some advice about what leadership should look like in a wicked problem context in the form of eight pithy maxims:

1 relationships not structures
2 reflection not reaction

3 positive deviance not negative acquiescence
4 negative capability
5 constructive dissent not destructive consent
6 collective intelligence not individual genius
7 community of fate not a fatalist community
8 empathy not egotism.

Point 1 is that rather than relying on given formal institutional decision-making structures, we need to develop strong relationships across the organisation and between organisations. An organisation is set up to solve particular types of problem and its formal structures reflect these problems. The far-reaching scope of a wicked challenge means that finding people who 'get' the issue wherever they are in terms of location in the organisation or seniority is more important.

Point 2 prompts us to abandon the Napoleonic model of the decisive leader for whom it is more important to act than what that action is. Rather we need to step back and ponder the nature of the problem facing us and start thinking in a wholly different way.

Points 3 and 5 suggest that we cannot afford to just go along with things as they have been, so we need to stand up and point out that things are different now and alert people to this. So our deviance and dissent is positive and constructive.

Negative capability (point 4) refers to an ability to live with uncertainty: to get involved, even though we cannot bring a clear solution or well established professional practices to bear on the case. We need to engage more to explore the dimensions of the issue.

Point 6 is that no one person can grasp the whole of the problem; rather, we need to get people thinking together, to facilitate a process where everyone's mind is working together.

The problem may seem vast and insuperable, but fatalism is not helpful – yet we must accept the community of others with whom we are fated by the problem to work together. We need to go into the situation thinking about the perspective of others and try and get inside that, through empathy, rather than seeing it as a context where we need to really assert our interests.

Arguably much of this advice is familiar; maybe it's good advice for many management situations. But it does point to the way that when tackling a wicked challenge we are operating outside the realm of routine management. We need a much more empathetic, reflective, creative approach. We think this is relevant to RDM, particularly at the beginnings of the institutional culture change it engenders. We would argue that most institutions remain at this stage. We would also emphasise that even if one is not a manager, one does have a role in leadership as understood here.

Exploring further

The aim of the chapter was to prompt you to think more about the nature of the managerial/leadership challenge that RDM poses. At the moment RDM is not 'business as usual'. In that context, everyone involved needs to operate in a somewhat different way from normal. It would be useful to reflect a little on people you have met in the RDM context and to think who stands out as a good role model. This might be someone who you work with or a colleague at another institution. Reflecting on what makes them stand out can point to some behaviours that are worth emulating.

Also reflect on how you yourself operate: can you do more to offer the type of leadership that RDM calls for? How can you develop the necessary attributes?

Further reading

If you want to read more about the idea of RDM as a wicked problem you could read the following works:

Cox, A. M., Pinfield, S. and Smith, J. (2016) Moving a Brick Building: UK libraries coping with RDM as a 'wicked' problem, *Journal of Librarianship and Information Science*, **48** (1), 3–17.

Awre, C., et al. (2015) Research Data Management as a 'wicked problem', *Library Review*, **64** (4/5), 356–71.

References

Cox, A. M., Pinfield, S. and Smith, J. (2016) Moving a Brick Building: UK libraries coping with research data management as a 'wicked' problem, *Journal of Librarianship and Information Science*, **48** (1), 3–17.

Grint, K. (2008) Wicked Problems and Clumsy Solutions: The role of leadership, *Clinical Leader*, **1** (2), 11–15.

Horn, R. E. and Weber, R. P. (2007) *New Tools for Resolving Wicked Problems: Mess mapping and resolution mapping processes*, Strategy Kinetics LLC, http://robertweber.typepad.com/strategykinetics/New_Tools_For_ Resolving_Wicked_Problems_Exec_Summary.pdf.

Rittel, H. W. and Webber, M. M. (1973) Dilemmas in a General Theory of Planning, *Policy Sciences*, **4** (2), 155–69.

CHAPTER 7

Research data services

Aims

The aim of this chapter is to explore the potential elements of a research data service(s) (RDS). It also sets this in a wider context of shifts in how research is supported as a whole in HE institutions.

Research data services (RDS)

Looking across the HE sector there seems to be a pattern towards developing services in areas where researchers need particular guidance and support. Following this trend, a central RDS may be created to take some of the burden of effort off researchers, apply special expertise and benefit from the economies to be gained of performing roles centrally. Such services can be understood as consisting of the following five components:

1 institutional policy
2 developing a clear and agreed mission
3 support, advice and training
4 infrastructure
5 evaluation strategy.

First, the task of defining an *institutional policy* on research data, backed by a business case, is likely to define the context within which the RDS can be built. A second component of an RDS is about *developing a clear and agreed mission*. A central aspect of this could be user requirements gathering at an initial stage. Specific services that can be developed are usefully grouped under the *support, advice and training* component and, as another component, *infrastructure*.

Support, advice and training
• Advocacy work – increasing understanding amongst the academic community and university leadership of the complex issues around RDM. This includes promoting awareness of policy. This is an important enough aspect of advocacy to be given special emphasis.
• Advice – from tailored one-to-one support through to generic FAQs and web pages. Supporting data management planning (DMP) is one specific aspect of an advisory service, but is important enough to often be seen as a service in itself. Hence in this book there is a chapter on data management planning.
• Training – this could be anything from one-to-one training to workshops, short courses, webinars and online tutorials.

Infrastructure
• Managing active data – this includes data storage, back-ups and data security.
• Appraisal and description of data for deposit, including data cataloguing. The catalogue may or may not be linked to a repository with access to data. It might be simply a listing of contact details and descriptions of datasets.
• Data sharing and long-term preservation.

Finally, the fifth component of the service is to develop an *evaluation strategy* capable of providing material to reflect the performance of the RDS, both at the level of the mission of the service as a whole, and for each individual part of it. Collectively these components make up an RDS. Later chapters will consider these areas in more detail.

The extent to which each of these components is developed will vary across institutions. Non-research-intensive institutions will probably have limited resources, and if so then work primarily at the policy level, combined with advocacy and self-help advice. This may be entirely appropriate if research is not the most central activity in the institution. Other institutions may focus more heavily on a wide range of technical or infrastructural services in response to the specific needs of the researcher community or the requirements of external funders.

Exploring further
Explore some institutional research data websites to see what kinds of services are being offered. Is the focus on softer support services or 'harder' technical services?

Vision, mission, strategy and governance

An RDS, like any organisational structure, needs a clearly defined and agreed purpose. This may evolve; indeed it is likely to do so, as its context changes. In particular, it will change in alignment with wider organisational and institutional strategies, in turn shaped by the wider changing environment. Classic ways of articulating purpose are:

- A vision, a short aspirational statement of what an organisation or service aspires to achieve, and set in the wider context. It is abstract, idealistic and future-oriented.
- A mission, a more detailed statement of the purpose of the organisational structure. It is more concrete, realistic and present-oriented.
- Strategic aims and objectives and specific plans lie beneath these.

These statements do not live in isolation. They are linked and aligned to other, wider strategies.

So far, much of this is standard management practice. It is important that these purposes are conceived in conversation with internal and external stakeholders. It is equally important that aspirations are balanced with available resources.

The scope and ambition of the mission of an RDS could be limited. It could simply be to ensure compliance with funder policy or manage the risk around non-compliance. It could also be much more aspirational and seek to promote open science and the free traffic of ideas, tied to an institutional research mission that aims to disseminate the university's research as widely as possible or to ensure the integrity of research undertaken.

Success against objectives needs to be evaluated. This is discussed in greater depth in Chapter 17.

Exploring further

For an institution you are interested in, consider what you think the RDS mission should be. Below are some possible elements of a mission statement for an RDS (deliberately not presented in a logical order).

Which statement seems best or can you rewrite and combine the text into an improved statement?

- 'To ensure compliance with the mandates of national and international funders of social science research.'
- 'To ensure compliance with the Concordat on Open Data.'
- 'To raise awareness of issues around RDM in the scholarly communities inside the institution.'
- 'To create a culture of open sharing of research data within institutional research communities.'
- 'To provide a robust and supportive infrastructure for storing, sharing and preserving research data.'
- 'To manage risk around changing funder demands in the context of competition for research funding.'
- 'To promote understanding of the benefits of open science.'
- 'To ensure that researchers have access to timely advice and support to meet their needs for RDM.'
- 'To ensure that researchers understand their responsibilities arising around RDM and are trained in the necessary skills.'
- 'To ensure all researchers have a well formulated and actively maintained data management plan.'
- 'To steward the research and research data of the communities of scholars at the university within the context of its mission to do world-class research with significant impact in areas of societal need.'
- 'To ensure data produced by the university's research is widely visible.'

These statements work at very different levels. Some stress compliance; some are more value-driven. Some seek to minimise risk; others are more expansive. Some place responsibility on the researcher; others take on some responsibility for the institution. All need to be defined more clearly as strategies with SMART objectives and a plan for evaluation (see Chapter 17).

You may have reflected that these statements can only be written in the context of related strategy documents and with an analysis of the institutional context.

When you have done this it is worth thinking about who you would involve in the discussion about the development of an RDS.

Try and make a list of people or roles that you would want to be involved in developing the RDM strategy.

Stakeholders

Agreeing on a vision and mission for the RDS implies bringing together key stakeholders to agree a strategy and review progress. This will involve:

- representatives of the academic community
- university leadership
- professional services with an interest in RDM, such as the library, IT and research administrators.

In addition, it is worth considering the point of view of a range of external stakeholders, such as:

- research funders
- research communities
- commercial partners.

Supporting research

As we discovered in Chapter 2, research is very important to universities, financially and symbolically. It is not surprising that specialist services to support research have been strengthened over time. One example is the emergence of central research administration departments which support the conduct of research by universities. They help researchers to secure funding and oversee the management of funded projects. They may also monitor research quality and integrity, including managing the process of approving research ethics. They may also input to researcher development, through various forms of training.

An important aspect of this trend to supporting research is the emergence of systems to do so. Current research information systems (CRIS) (also known as research information management systems or RIMS) are a class of system for managing projects, researcher profiles and their outputs. These systems track research projects, including research funding both pre- and post-award. They may also track project-related activities such as impact, public engagement and dissemination activities, as well as publications and other research outputs, and the preparation for and submission to national research assessments; but these functions may also be performed by specialised systems. These systems often interact with bibliographic services such as Scopus or the Web of Science to identify publications; and they often interact with institutional repositories to manage deposit of open-access versions of research outputs. This allows institutions to monitor research activity and productivity; they can also be seen as tools of managerial control. Research data is likely to become another aspect of research activity and productivity that such systems will seek to track.

A parallel trend that provides another important context to RDS is the way that university libraries are increasingly providing a range of support to research as such. Libraries have focused very much on supporting students in the last few decades, and information literacy training in this context has become central to professional identity. Recognition that researchers were using the physical library less frequently, if at all, and that they were perhaps taking for granted what is provided digitally, not linking the provision of these digital services to the academic library that provides them, has led in the last decade to a shift in the balance of support back to research. Libraries have begun developing services such as:

- *Open access*. This revolves around promoting the benefits of making research outputs openly available, as well as encouraging researchers to think through copyright and ownership issues around their work. It also involves running an institutional repository for research outputs and promoting the visibility of its content.
- *Information literacy* for researchers and support to do literature reviews.
- *Bibliometric or research analytics services*. These revolve around helping researchers understand metrics such as journal impact factors and researcher h-indexes and promoting the responsible use of metrics to measure and improve the quality and impact of research. This is likely to involve explaining the value of altmetrics and helping researchers to devise strategies to increase the visibility of their work through social media. This could also be linked to supporting researchers to maximise the impact of their work in general.
- *Scholarly presses or hosting services*. This is about providing the infrastructure through which academics can set up new journals to publish the latest research in their field, through to providing

publishing services that may include the sale and dissemination of print copies of journals, conference proceedings, edited books, monographs and grey literature.

- *Collection development and reference enquiries* – a more familiar role of guiding researchers to find the information they need, and ensuring that the library's collection meets the needs of the institution's researcher community.

As a result of this strengthening focus, libraries have started to establish units that are dedicated to research support. Many reflect deeper changes in the nature of scholarship in the digital era. This shift to thinking more about how to support research in academic libraries is a profound one. Lorcan Dempsey (2016) has pointed to the way that the library shifts from an outside-in role, in which it obtains resources from the wider world for its inner communities of scholars, to an inside-out role, where the role shifts to stewarding material created by the scholars within the institution and making that knowledge visible to the wider world. The services mentioned above, including open access and RDM, fit in this paradigm.

If the library is supporting RDM, it may well be as part of a unit that offers such services to research. This is important, because it prompts us to consider the linkages between RDM and these other areas of activity. For example, the link between RDM and open access/open data is strong, but the agendas are a little different (as discussed in Chapter 5). Metrics for data are likely to become more and more important, so connecting the bibliometrics service with the RDM service may make sense.

Exploring further

It is a useful activity to revisit the websites of some universities to explore the services they are offering researchers and consider how they are being promoted. We will look more systematically at this in Chapter 11.

Further reading

Not surprisingly, there has been quite a lot of literature around developing RDS. Four very useful edited books are:

Johnston, L. R. (2017a) *Curating Research Data: Volume One: Practical strategies for your digital repository*, ACRL.

Johnston, L. R. (2017b) *Curating Research Data, Volume Two: A handbook of current practice*, ACRL.

Pryor, G. (ed.) (2012) *Managing Research Data*, Facet Publishing.

Pryor, G., Jones, S. and Whyte, A. (eds) (2013) *Delivering Research Data Management Services: Fundamentals of good practice*, Facet Publishing.

Ray, J. M. (ed.) (2014) *Research Data Management: Practical strategies for information professionals*, Purdue University Press.

Some other readings are:

Akers, K. G., Sferdean, F. C., Nicholls, N. H. and Green, J. A. (2014) Building Support for Research Data Management: Biographies of eight research universities, *International Journal of Digital Curation*, **9** (2), 171–91.

There are many published case studies of institutions starting RDS. In this paper Akers et al. try to map out some patterns in how RDS develop in practice (mostly from a library perspective).

The *International Journal of Digital Curation* (www.ijdc.net) is probably one you will want to bookmark, as it is an open-access journal publishing many articles on RDM.

For examples of many key types of documents refer to:

Fearon, D., Gunia, B., Lake, S., Pralle, B. and Sallans, A. (2013) *Research Data Management Services*, SPEC Kit 334, Washington, DC: Association of Research Libraries.

A series of reports looking at how RDM is being implemented in practice in different institutions has been produced by OCLC:

Bryant, R., Lavoie, B. and Malpas, C. (2017–) The Realities of Research Data Management, OCLC, www.oclc.org/research/publications/2017/oclcresearch-research-data-management.html.

References

Dempsey, L. (2016) Library Collections in the Life of the User: Two directions, *LIBER Quarterly*, **26** (4), http://dx.doi.org/10.18352/lq.10170.

CHAPTER 8

Staffing a research data service

Aims

The aim of this chapter is to help you think through the staffing issues around supporting research data management and for a research data service.

New activities and roles

A greater focus on RDM implies some new activities, such as preparing data to be shared or providing training. Or it could imply a redistribution of activities, e.g. from the researcher to someone in an RDS. It may create wholly new roles, especially in the support area or in running a repository. Logically, this creation or redistribution of work can be met in a number of ways:

1 Research teams themselves may take on new tasks, be that the principal investigator or research assistants, e.g. taking on primary responsibility for data management in a project or documenting data at the end of the project.

2 Existing local support staff might take on a role; for example, if an academic department has an IT specialist or someone who helps write project proposals, they might take on some roles associated with RDM. They might offer day-to-day support around storing active data or help write a data management plan.

3 Existing central support staff could add a new role – be they in the library, IT, records management, research administration, staff development, or in a number of other departments. Such new roles could involve anything from adding some slides about RDM to a briefing on information literacy through to running a data repository. This could be on the basis of their existing knowledge and skills or by them having some retraining and upskilling. It might be that a few

people have their job significantly changed, or that tasks are widely distributed across a large number of staff in different teams.

4 The organisation could employ new staff to take on the role; perhaps even in a new organisational structure. For example, a new co-ordinator might be appointed to ensure that all the professional services supporting RDM are moving in the same direction.

Logically there are three other possibilities:

1 Some new activities created in the context of RDM are met collaboratively across a number of institutions. For example, it could be that a local cross-institutional network could take on training of researchers in RDM.
2 Some work could be outsourced to a commercial provider. For example, the role of providing secure long-term storage and preservation could be outsourced to a commercial vendor, who would be providing this service to a number of institutions.
3 Finally, another logical possibility is that tasks that could be undertaken by a human are in fact built into processes/IT systems that effectively do this work. An example might be tools to automatically create metadata about research data, which relieves people of the need to create metadata manually.

It is highly probable, in fact, that almost all of these things will happen. So the effect of RDM is not simply to create a new job, it will subtly change many other jobs, and reconfigure the relationships between different professional groups.

It is generally accepted that no one part of an organisation has all the knowledge and skills to offer the complete RDS. It is likely to be a collaborative effort. However, the exact pattern seems to be highly variable between organisations, depending on existing practices and institutional structures, staff capabilities and mindsets and available services and technologies. The pattern is also likely to change over time, with one probable trend being towards routinisation and technology replacing skilled work.

Perhaps the approach will be primarily to place the onus on the research staff themselves to take up the tasks. Perhaps the focus will be on a central team or perhaps on distributed support.

This all sounds quite abstract but helps us think clearly about the overall impact of RDM on staffing in an organisation.

Exploring further

In Figure 8.1 we have set out some of the new tasks that RDM could potentially create. For each, consider who you think should take on the task: this could be on the basis of the institution you know about, such as the one you work for. Or you could just consider it in relation to your understanding of the specialist knowledge of the groups listed along the top row of the table.

For each task allot 6 points. If it is wholly to be the responsibility of one group give them 6 points, but you can distribute the points among a number of groups – for example, you might decide that training should be shared between IT and the library, so give them each 3 points. If you consider that it is not a role that should be undertaken simply score it zero.

You might want to also consider whether any of the tasks can be offered collaboratively or outsourced.

	Researchers	Library - specify team	Archives/ Records	IT	Research Office	Others (specify)
1 Writing an institutional policy						
2 RDS requirements gathering through a survey						
3 RDS requirements gathering through curation profile						
4 Monitoring of funder policies						
5 Guidance and support for data management						
6 Management of active research data						
7 Information security						
8 Practical data management advice						
9 Advocacy including raising awareness of funders' policies						
10 Maintenance of a guidance website						

	Researchers	Library - *specify*	Archives/ Records	IT	Research Office	Others *specify*
11 Guidance and support for staff and students						
12 Training for staff and students						
13 Advice on management of sensitive research						
14 Advice on copyright and licensing of data						
15 Running the research data repository						
16 Running a metadata catalogue						
17 Documenting processes						
18 Creating metadata for research data						
19 Selecting data for deposit						
20 Ensuring that locally deposited data is visible in national services						
21 Integration of locally deposited research data into the local discovery infrastructure						
22 Monitoring re-use/ citation of data in repository						
23 Data preservation						
24 Promotion of knowledge of sources of re-usable data						
25 Promotion of data sharing and knowledge of national data repository services						
26 Overall leadership on RDM						

Figure 8.1 *Continued*

As well as giving you an insight into the different tasks created around RDM, the exercise helps you see clearly where the burden of supporting RDM might lie. It also helps you see how different people will have to work together on some shared tasks.

We have often used the chart as part of our courses and the result is usually that when people compare their answers they see that different institutions take rather different approaches. One size does not fit all. There are a number of reasons for this:

- Since communities of researchers have different degrees of readiness for RDM, depending on the mix of research fields represented in the institution, so the need for support will be different.
- Institutions already operate differently in terms of how professional services are structured and their exact remit. For example, it could be that the staff development department might take on all staff induction and training, so RDM sits naturally there. In other institutions this could happen across other professional services.
- If one section sees RDM as a strategic priority they may well wish to take on a leadership role, and where there is ambiguity about who could undertake a task they will be dynamic about taking it on. Other sections may be under pressure from other directions and simply not have the energy or resources to bring to RDM.
- It also depends simply on how events play out and internal politics.

Who does what?

While one size does not fit all institutions, we can make some general observations about which groups are likely to have strengths in which particular aspects of RDM.

1 Researchers themselves – it is obvious that researchers have the most immediate knowledge of their research data and a direct interest in how it is shared and preserved. Only they can really do the planning across the lifecycle to ensure that data are managed successfully. They will be the best to develop metadata to describe research data, because they have in-depth subject knowledge. They may also be best able to contribute to decisions on what data should be preserved. In large projects, there may be separate roles for data managers or specialists to analyse data.

2 Senior research managers – with an overview of research activity and an eye to research quality, senior research managers will have a clear understanding of the balance of incentives for RDM as it plays out for

the subject disciplines they have responsibility for. It would also be unwise to leave the voice of senior research managers out of consideration of overall strategy and policy. Of course, they are unlikely to be interested in the detail of procedures and processes.

3 Research administrators – many universities have a central research administration team. They often have overall responsibility for: understanding the funding landscape; supporting funding proposal writing; managing grant funds; research quality and integrity, including research ethics; training researchers; training and experience of PhD students. It is obvious that such professionals have a lot to contribute to the discussion about RDM, given this deep involvement in research from before even a clear idea for a project has been developed, through writing a proposal, to complying with funder guidelines about data sharing at the end of a project. It is quite probable that the first time a researcher will think about RDM is when they see the need to write a DMP for a research proposal. If that is the case they may well go to central research administration for help as their very first port of call.

4 The IT service – since IT supplies the basic infrastructure within which most research is done, again it is obvious that the IT service will have an important part to play. When the researcher suddenly realises how much data they are generating in a project and encounters data storage problems or when they want to share data securely with project partners, at that point they will naturally turn to the IT service for support. Developing a system for capturing metadata is also something the IT service might lead on. Thus aspects of active data storage, security and data integrity all seem to fall under the remit of the IT service.

5 The library – again many aspects of RDM seem to relate to quite familiar library roles. One example would be locating data for re-use which is analogous to any form of search for literature. Libraries have long had a remit around preservation. Above all, perhaps, because of their role in open access and often in running an institutional repository for research outputs, they will be seen as having a part to play in RDM. This could be in promoting data sharing through advocacy, defining collection management plans or providing metadata services for material being placed in a data repository. Librarians' commitment to open standards and experience of building

discovery infrastructure equip them to make an important contribution around making research data deposits widely visible.

6 Archives and records management – many of the principles for data curation are based on fundamental archival principles. The archives or records managers in the institution may well play a pivotal role in RDM, e.g. in understanding the issues around digital preservation.

7 Distributed support services – many academic departments have IT staff, research administrators and information professionals working at the local level. They already provide close support to researchers. They are well positioned therefore to provide daily support with specific issues and can be a channel to promote aspects of RDM.

From this brief summary we can see that there is likely to be input from a number of professional groups around RDM.

Exploring further
Go back to your rating of the different tasks in the chart in Figure 8.1 and in the light of the discussion consider whether you want to change the weightings given to different groups.

Discuss your scoring with a colleague from a different organisation or background. For example, if you work in an institution already, talk to someone in a different professional service. How does their perspective differ?

The collaborative research data service

It seems clear that RDM is likely to be a collaborative enterprise between researchers themselves and professional services, probably including the research administration, IT and library. The focus could be on a central hub of support. It might be based in the library, IT or administration or be a separate unit. Another model would be to focus on distributed professional staff to promote understanding of key issues.

If it is likely to be a multi-professional service this implies a number of challenges that will need to be addressed:

• **Different professional perspectives.** There is a literature, for example, exploring the contrasting cultures of librarians and IT staff (Favini, 1997). They do tend to think in rather different ways. At the risk of stereotyping, IT staff tend to focus on technology, whereas librarians have more of a people focus. Working out how to combine these orientations will be key.

- **Organisational boundaries.** Communicating across organisational boundaries is always challenging, quite apart from 'cultural' differences between different groups. Trying to work outside established communication channels and management lines will cause problems.
- **A dedicated unit for RDM** drawing on staff from all three groups could be created, but would itself sit outside usual institutional structures, and so in the long run might have quite weak influence.

New skills and roles

One of the most interesting areas is to consider completely new roles that may be created around RDM. A few examples might be:

- A **research data co-ordinator** is someone with a remit to manage change in the organisation as a whole, perhaps within a temporary project. The end point may be to experiment with organisational structures and services to support RDM. As a change agent they need a good **research data co-ordinator** understanding of the institutional environment, and good powers of negotiation and influencing.
- A **data curator** is a specialist in the more 'technical' issues around data preservation. Given wider issues around digital preservation across institutions, this might not just be for research data.
- A **research tool support specialist** might be more about helping researchers pick tools for data management, analysis or visualisation. They might themselves be experts able to conduct analysis. This is a role that is somewhat hybrid between research and support, with a strong technical skillset. They might be involved in evaluating, procuring and training a whole range of tools for researchers, not just data management tools.

Another interesting perspective on new roles is the idea of 'embedded roles', e.g. a support professional embedded in a department, research group or project team with a special remit for RDM. The strength of the embedded role is the depth of the relationship with researchers and the specialist knowledge they have to support a particular group. Such roles are likely to be fascinating; yet to work effectively they must have strong communication channels back to the professional service in which they are ultimately based.

Exploring further

Do some desk research to analyse where the RDS sits in some institutions. You might pick different types of institution to see if there are differences or pick ones similar to the one where you work or are studying. Where does the RDS sit in the organisation? How does it relate to established services like IT, research administration and the library? If within one of these services, who does it report to? How many staff does it have and what do the job titles suggest about the range of roles there are? Is it a one-man band or a large team? If available, you can look at the background of current job holders to see what kinds of skills they are bringing to their role.

If you get the chance to talk to people working in RDM ask about their history in the field. It is often a complex one: but it is always fascinating to find out about people's career journeys.

Further reading

The following study by the authors looks at the professional relations around RDM and how these can be conceptualised:

Verbaan, E. and Cox, A. M. (2014) Occupational Sub-Cultures, Jurisdictional Struggle and Third Space: Theorising professional service responses to research data management, *Journal of Academic Librarianship*, **40** (3–4), 211–19.

Although only one aspect of RDM, the following paper explores how data curators saw their own roles:

Kouper, I. (2016) Professional Participation in Digital Curation, *Library and Information Science Research*, **38** (3), 212–23.

References

Favini, R. (1997) *The Library and Academic Computing Center: Cultural perspectives and recommendations for improved interaction* (ACRL white paper), www.ala.org/acrl/publications/whitepapers/nashville/favini.

CHAPTER 9

Requirements gathering for a research data service

Aims

The aim of this chapter is to explore how to identify the requirements for an RDS in an institution. It will help you think through what you would want to learn about user needs from an RDS and how to gather such information.

Finding out more about an institution

Throughout the book so far we have prompted you to talk to researchers about research and research data as a way of starting to build your own deeper understanding of the issues. This is solid groundwork for developing an intuition for what types of service are needed.

At some point you may well want to gather evidence more systematically as a foundation for making decisions about services. Of course, one cannot simply ask about what services people want. It is hard for 'users' to imagine what services there could be. We will be thinking more about what they need, based on an examination of existing practice. But in any case systematic data will be invaluable for working out the appropriate service for the needs of your institution. Systematic evidence will certainly help you in influencing others about the direction the service should take. As it will be an inherently collaborative challenge for a number of professional services working with researchers themselves, you will need an evidence base to persuade others what the service should look like.

There are a number of other advantages to undertaking such a study. It might seem that senior research leaders in the institution will already know the situation in their faculty or department. Actually, they are probably as uncertain about current data practices as anyone else. They will probably be extremely interested in the results of any study. They can help themselves to identify potential problem areas. Undertaking the formal task of having a project to study user needs will help assemble stakeholders and get them working together. It will identify problem areas but it will also help you identify pathfinders and examples of good practice.

An evidence-gathering process itself will also be a means to inform users, alerting them to the existence of an institutional issue they may not have thought about. As the first step in a change management process an evidence-gathering exercise could itself have a powerful effect. Thus, simply inserting a question in the survey asking respondents about their awareness of local policy alerts them to the existence of the policy, as well as gauging its visibility before the survey. It should also help researchers on the ground start to identify who has institutional responsibility.

Probably the most cost-effective way to gather evidence is going to be a web-based questionnaire. Ideally this should be combined with qualitative data collection through interviews and focus groups.

Exploring further

Thinking about an institution you are interested in, who are the key stakeholders in this evidence-gathering process?

What approach to data gathering do you feel most comfortable with? A questionnaire can reach a lot of people, but interviews or focus groups really allow you to dig deeply into the issues. If you want to collect both forms of data, there are logics for doing a survey first and for doing interviews first. Doing a survey first gives you an overview of current practices; you can dig deeper into 'why' through interviews. The questionnaire can help you identify problem areas which need further investigation. Basing the questionnaire on the interviews allows you to make sure you formulate the questions in a way that will be understood.

Surveys
Planning
The Digital Asset Framework (DAF) is a good starting point for thinking about how to plan your user requirements study. It has been developed over a number of years and used by many institutions. The latest version of the toolkit is a good starting point for planning your study (Johnson, Parsons and Chiarelli, 2016).

A number of decisions need to be made:

- Timing. Response rates will be affected by when the questionnaire is distributed. Busy times of year like the beginning of the teaching year or exam times are obviously to be avoided. Equally, it makes sense not to try and conduct the study when everyone is on holiday in August.
- Survey platform. There are a range of cheap or free survey platforms to host your questionnaire.
- Channels for distributing the questionnaire. Investing time in getting a good response rate is important. Some sort of senior management endorsement for the importance of responding is useful, but could be hard to negotiate. It may be of value to offer an incentive for completing the questionnaire.
- Baseline data. It will be useful to get hold of baseline data on the numbers of staff at different levels of seniority by department.

Most of the chapter focuses on potential questions, because reflecting on these gives you the clearest idea of the kind of information you might want to collect.

Survey design

Asking the right questions is going to be key to the value of the survey. But it is always going to be hard to get a wording and logic that works for everyone. As we have seen the very word 'data' is off-putting for many researchers, so a survey entitled 'Research Data Management' has the potential to immediately alienate some potential respondents! If you ask someone whether they want training in documenting research data they may well agree, but disagree if you offer them training in metadata. Ultimately there is no answer to this dilemma, but piloting the survey with researchers will help you hone the wording.

A related issue is that research data practices are often so complex that it will be hard for a researcher to answer sensibly. For example, if they have been researching in a particular field for 10 years and have had half-a-dozen projects, how can they easily answer a question about the amount of data they have or how they store it? Storage infrastructures have changed rapidly in the last decade, so sensible storage practices from 10 years ago seem quaint. It may make sense, therefore, to word the questions to ask the researcher about one of their main current projects, rather than ask about everything they do or have done.

Probably your survey will cover: research data types/amount, data management practices, training needs and attitudes. We will discuss each of these in some depth.

Demographics

It is essential to have some information about the individuals completing the survey, such as: department; job title/status.

It is going to be important to look at the response rate from different departments, because you will want to be able to report results at this level or at least by faculty. We know RDM practices vary very much across disciplines and meta-disciplines, so understanding the survey requires us to look at variations by subject. Seniority is also important to consider. We expect PhD students to have somewhat different attitudes and expectations from those of senior researchers. Failing to take such differences into account when analysing the results is going to give us quite a misleading picture of the meaning of the survey. That is obvious, but few of the published studies actually offer this analysis.

You might also want to ask about funders that the researchers are working with. In a big institution the range of funders that researchers work with is amazing. Funders have different RDM policies, so you want to know who the key funders for your researchers are.

Perhaps you could also ask about gender, since you may think there will be variations in behaviour and attitude. If you are asking about gender remember to word the question sensitively, with options such as gender variant/non-conforming. You might want to ask about how long the individual has been in the institution, because this could affect awareness of policy and other attitudes.

Such demographic questions can come at the beginning or the end of the survey. Sometimes it is more engaging to start with the substantive questions, before going through the demographics later on.

Research data types and amounts

Common types of question are about the types of data researchers collect, be that based on methodology or file types (documents, spreadsheets, etc.). You might want to ask about non-digital data types too. Chapter 3 summarised this question. When we did the study at Sheffield many respondents said they had six or more forms of data, immediately alerting us to the complexity of the issue. You might want to ask people to identify any forms of sensitive data they handle, be that personal information or commercially sensitive material.

You might also ask about the amount of data researchers have. It might be more reasonable to ask about how much they are expecting to collect for their current main project. They may well have no real idea. When we did the survey at Sheffield around 25% of people said don't know. This is a good gauge of the spread of data management planning.

Another question in this section could be about who is likely to use the data, e.g. including researchers in the institution or beyond and the public.

Data management
It will be useful to ask researchers where they store their data. The full range of options will vary by institution, but is likely to include:

- local hard drive of own computer or laptop
- external hard drive
- university network storage
- departmental intranet
- a commercial cloud service.

The plethora of storage locations in use is a particular problem for security, so discovering what locations are in use can be very helpful.

As regards backing up research data, one can ask about what is backed up and frequency:

- daily
- weekly
- ad hoc
- never
- don't know
- other.

Finally in this section, you might well want to ask about whether people have a data management plan. Of course, even here terminology is quite variable, so you will have to give an approximate explanation of what a data management plan is.

Service awareness and use

Part of the questionnaire could discover awareness and use of existing local, national and international services. So you might want to ask about awareness of local policy, local RDS (including any repository) and subject repositories such as Github. The DAF toolkit has a useful list of possible repositories. You might also want to ask them about their awareness of relevant research funder policy. You could simply ask them if they know the policy of their current funder (if any).

Training

You may well want to ask researchers what training needs they identify for themselves. The list below suggests some of the areas you might want to ask them about (see also Chapter 15). These data will help target your training offering, especially if you can identify different needs by faculty or seniority.

- storing research data
- developing a research data management plan
- copyright and intellectual property relating to data
- documenting your research
- citing research data
- sharing your research data
- funders' requirements and RDM
- creating metadata for research data
- ethics and consent.

Attitudes to RDM and data sharing

An interesting question might be to ask respondents to rate research data management as a problem and ask them to identify what they think are the main challenges. Options for the latter could include:

- data quality
- lack of data sharing
- licensing restrictions
- lack of standards
- difficulty locating existing data sources
- data security.

This will give you a sense of where people are already seeing problems.

You might also want to dig deeper into researcher attitudes to sharing research data. Here you could draw on the work of Tenopir et al. (2011; 2015), who have surveyed researchers about their attitudes towards data sharing, enabling you to compare local findings with that of published surveys. Thus you might ask about their willingness to use other people's data, their willingness to share data with or without restrictions, and what they see as the main barriers for them to share their data. The latter will give you a good feel for where demand for a repository service might come from.

Interpreting the results

Making sense of your results may not be as straightforward as you might first think.

You will want to look closely at the response rate. This means having baseline data, e.g. the total number of research active staff at different levels of seniority in different departments. If your responses are skewed towards PhD students or if only a small proportion of researchers in one faculty respond, this could give very misleading results if you do not take that into account.

Even if you get a good, balanced response rate to your survey there is non-response bias: the kind of people who fill in surveys may not be like those who do not, meaning that the replies do not represent the views of the wider population. It is probable that the kind of person who fills in a survey about RDM is either good at it or worried about it. Actually, the most in need of support might be those who do not recognise the issue. There are technical ways to deal with non-response, such as to interview a sample of people who did not respond to the questionnaire to see if they would have replied consistently with those who did actually respond. Probably you will not want to go this far, but this kind of consideration should make you cautious about relying too heavily on the results.

Another problem is that if you want to benchmark your findings against previous studies at other institutions there are a number of issues:

- There is little standardisation of questions across surveys. Slight differences in wording can lead to different results.
- Ironically, the raw data from previous studies has rarely been shared. You are relying on published reports, which may not give exact figures.

- Few previous studies break down results by subject discipline or seniority. So most published studies simply report the total responses per institution, without differentiating subject areas. Even if they did, of course, there is no certainty that the department of X in one institution is really comparable to a department of X in another, since subject disciplines are too messy to make such easy comparisons. We also really need to cross-analyse between seniority and response. Again, virtually no previous published studies do this.

Exploring further
Now is a good point to stop and reflect on what you really need to know. The shorter your questionnaire the higher the response rate is likely to be.

Start thinking about what questions you think are essential. Also give some thought to the nuances of wording. How are you going to name the survey? How are you going to define research data, so that people understand what are relevant responses? Will you ask people to focus on their current or most recent project – or try and summarise their 'normal' practice?

If you are in the position to do so, talk to other stakeholders such as research leaders or other professional services to see what they want to know from a questionnaire.

You can see a long list of possible questions in the DAF toolkit and the ones used at Sheffield in the appendix to the paper by Cox and Williamson (2015).

Interviews and focus groups

If you get a good response, a questionnaire will give you a convincing snapshot of behaviour and opinion across the whole institution. But the more exploratory possibilities of qualitative data collection techniques such as interviews and focus groups could be important because:

- The whole question of what are and what are not research data is unclear.
- Because their current behaviours are complex, it can be hard to ask questions that reflect nuances in behaviour or for respondents to fully reflect what they are doing.
- It's hard to give simple answers to questions about motivation, e.g. asking about why one might not share data is quite hard to answer.

- Where people are unfamiliar with an issue their reflections on their own behaviour and motivation can be unreliable.
- The most problematic issues are complex. If RDM is a wicked problem, its complexity and interconnections make it hard to ask about in the structured, preset questionnaire.

Thus, it makes sense to combine a survey with qualitative methods. The drawback, of course, is that it is much more time-consuming, so realistically the approach will have to be much more selective.

Chapter 3 already referred to the data curation profile interview. This is a very structured approach to asking a researcher about a particular dataset. At the other end of the spectrum a much more open-ended approach might be taken in talking to a researcher. This is likely to start with an open-ended discussion of the researcher's research work and gradually lead into some more specific areas such as funding, data collection, data processing and publishing. But your interview guide may be quite open-ended, allowing you to explore researchers' experience in a very open way.

Exploring further

Start thinking about what you would most like to ask in your interviews and focus groups.

There is an increasing amount of literature about the variations between disciplines in research practices. This should be a fairly reliable guide to broad practices in particular disciplinary areas and so is a good starting point. See if you can find some published literature on a field of interest to you.

Further reading

The Digital Asset Framework was created as a method for gathering data about an institution, including suggested wording for interviews and questionnaires. The following report supplies an update of the survey aspect of this method.

Johnson, R., Parsons, T. and Chiarelli, A. (2016) *JISC Data Asset Framework Toolkit*, https://zenodo.org/record/177876#.

Many studies based on surveys of individual institutions have been published. The one conducted at Sheffield also asks questions about the method itself.

Cox, A. M. and Williamson, L. (2015) The 2014 DAF Survey at the University of Sheffield, *International Journal of Digital Curation*, **10** (1), 210–29.

References

Tenopir, C., Allard, S., Douglass, K., Aydinoglu, A. U., Wu, L., Read, E., Manoff, M. and Frame, M. (2011) Data Sharing by Scientists: Practices and perceptions, *PLOS ONE*, **6** (6), e21101.

Tenopir, C., Dalton, E. D., Allard, S., Frame, M., Pjesivac, I., Birch, B., Pollock, D. and Dorsett, K. (2015) Changes in Data Sharing and Data Reuse Practices and Perceptions Among Scientists Worldwide, *PLOS ONE*, **10** (8), e0134826.

CHAPTER 10

Institutional policy and the business case for research data services

Aims

The aim of this chapter is to discuss aspects of developing and using an RDM policy.

Writing a policy

A policy is a written statement of general principles that guides activities and decision making on a particular issue across an organisation. Going through the process of bringing together key stakeholders (or their representatives) to agree on a common stance lays the essential foundation for a co-ordinated response to an issue. The very process of agreeing a policy helps solidify the issue, co-ordinate views on how it should be understood and clarify the stance of the institution.

Having the written policy in place motivates and aligns action, and reduces misunderstanding. At its heart is a definition of roles and responsibilities for key stakeholders. It is the mandate for any services the institution offers.

Developing a policy

An internal policy discussion to make a policy establishes that RDM is a recognised concern for the institution. Indeed, simply establishing that there is a need for a policy may be the first battle. As we saw in Chapter 6, some responses to a wicked challenge could be that 'there is no issue' or that 'it is adequately covered by existing policy or good practice'. Bringing key stakeholders together at a high level enables the institution to understand the full ramifications of the issue.

Because RDM touches on researchers at different levels and a number of professional support services there is a particular need to clarify roles.

It might be that writing the policy is the first action of an institution to respond to RDM; but it might be that pilot services need to be developed to prove the nature of the need.

Researching the policy is likely to involve data gathering in six areas:

1 The wider trends in the sector around RDM, e.g. why it has become a key issue.
2 More specifically, the wider policy context: what are the key current policies from governments, relevant funders and so on, with which local policy must align? What are the relevant legal reference points, e.g. in relation to data protection or copyright?
3 The state of play within the institution, to scope out the nature of the challenge, and to identify existing activities and resources. RDM as a label may be relatively new, but managing data has been going on for many years. So what are the kinds of actual issues the institution has? This work is described in the previous chapter.
4 The institutional mission, and how the issue around RDM touches on this. In a research-intensive institution, the link between RDM and research integrity will be core. In other institutions where research is perhaps a subsidiary activity to teaching, research may be seen as underlying particular institutional objectives, e.g. staff development or teaching quality. This will clearly affect how RDM is viewed, and so the tenor of the policy.
5 Other related institutional policies, to see how far the issue is already addressed and how the new policy will nest into existing policies, such as those on research integrity and ethics, open access, intellectual property rights, information security and digital preservation.
6 RDM policies in other institutions. Since many institutions already have such policies, there is little need to start the process with a blank piece of paper.

This research will make it possible to write a business case for RDM. The business case will identify the institution's readiness, the nature of the benefits of an RDS, the risks associated with not having an RDS of some form, and the costs. Institutions often have templates for a business case, that help in being as specific as possible about what the benefits are, who will benefit, when, and how to measure such benefits. Wherever possible these can be calculated in financial terms and set against the costs of a planned service.

The process of consultation will need to involve a number of key stakeholders:

- research leaders
- research administrators
- IT
- the library
- the archival team
- the legal team.

In practical terms, the general advice is that an individual or group then writes a draft policy, which is then circulated for comment in written form.

Exploring further

Find some existing institutional RDM policies. They could be from the institution you work for or have an interest in, and comparable institutions.

Undertake a close comparison of the policies. How are they structured? Look for common ground and differences. What common reference points are there? Do these relate to quoting wider policy statements or standards? Considering the differences, how far do these seem to relate simply to different institutional styles of presentation and how far to genuine differences in the underlying thinking itself?

Content of a policy

An RDM policy is likely to include the following elements:

- A title.
- A formal statement of scope and purpose.
- A definition of research data, be that in abstract terms or a listing of types of data. This is essential to explaining the scope to those uncertain about whether their work falls under the remit of the policy. Research itself may need to be defined, e.g. whether to include service evaluation activities.
- A broad articulation of the institution's stance on RDM. This might emphasise open data, but is more likely to simply assert the importance of RDM. At some level it will align with wider institutional objectives (e.g. it could link to a university's identity as a

world-leading research institution with a commitment to research integrity).
• Links to other related policies.
• A statement about why RDM is important.
• Roles and responsibilities. A key aspect of the document is to identify groups and their specific responsibilities relating to RDM. On the one hand the policy will say something about researchers' responsibilities; on the other, it will state in broad terms what support the institution offers in terms of services. In general the primary responsibility to handle and manage data effectively is likely to be placed on the lead researcher. The policy may give quite a lot of detail about their responsibilities or simply state this at a high level. It could identify the role of research leaders to make staff aware of their responsibilities. The policy may also make some mention of expectations about what happens in collaborative projects with other institutions. It will identify the types of service the institution offers to support RDM. Few policies seem to define which service department is responsible for providing particular services, but it will give the scope in terms of advice, training and infrastructure.
• Many policies also emphasise the need to write the costs of RDM into research proposals.

There will also be other standard elements, such as:

• a statement of ownership of the policy.
• a version number, date when the policy was published, and a date for review (probably a quite short time period given the dynamic nature of the issue).

Some of the content is likely to echo the wording in wider statements and sets of principles, e.g. definitions of data by other bodies.

One critical point of difference in RDM policies is around whether the primary thrust is to draw researchers' attention to their responsibilities as a means of managing risk or whether there is a strong emphasis on providing an infrastructure to encourage more active engagement with RDM.

Another critical point where policies are likely to differ between institutions is in terms of the strength of the commitment to data sharing.

In some policies the main focus is that data is managed carefully in every context. In contrast, in other policies there is a stronger focus on the notion of data sharing, even open access as an expectation. The latter implies responsibilities for the researcher to provide appropriate metadata and responsibilities for the institution to provide an infrastructure for data storage and preservation.

The following are some other areas of variation:

- It might assert the need for all research to have a DMP, or limit this to funded research.
- It might define default data retention periods.
- It is likely to provide guidance on the treatment of student-conducted research, potentially Masters and Undergraduate as well as PhD research.

A policy might make a statement about the ownership of research data, e.g. that it is the default that all data is owned by the university unless contracts with external funders stipulate otherwise.

Exploring further

Having thought about content, now consider the policies you have to hand, in terms of style, both of wording and visual look. How do the documents differ and which stylistic features seem most effective in the context of the purpose of the policy?

Layout and style

A policy will mirror the layout and style of other institutional policies. But there are some general principles that seem to make for effective policy presentation:

- use of direct language (rather than legalistic language or jargon)
- use of an active voice
- short sentences
- bullet points and lists
- clear structure
- plenty of white space
- keeping the document relatively concise.

Specific aspects such as names of individuals or particular services do not generally appear in policies, since they go quickly out of date.

Using and updating the RDM policy

Writing and agreeing on a policy is only the beginning. Having published the policy, it needs to be widely communicated to those affected. The policy is the mandate for services, so the question becomes:

- How are researcher responsibilities to be communicated?
- How is conformance to be monitored and possibly enforced, if at all?
- How will staff be given the requisite training?
- How in practice are institutional commitments to be realised?
- Who is responsible for achieving these changes?

Given the dynamic nature of RDM, the policy will need to be regularly reviewed, particularly in the early days after its creation.

Developing RDS is the subject of the following chapters.

CHAPTER 11

Support and advice for RDM

Aims

The aim of this chapter is to consider the requirements for an effective support and advice service for RDM, especially designing its web presence.

Offering support and advice

A core aspect of an RDS will be to provide information, support and advice to researchers in a timely and reliable manner. Providing a good support and advice service is challenging for a number of reasons:

1 Researchers' issues are inevitably diverse, reflecting the wide range of research practices in different fields.
2 Their issues are likely to be quite technical and couched in very specific forms related to a specific research project. In offering advice RDS staff are unlikely to fully understand the research objective or the wider norms of the research culture within which the research is being conducted.
3 The timing of when issues are likely to be raised is unpredictable. A project idea can be developed at any time, so requests for information, while they will reflect cycles of activity for research, cannot be easily predicted. A request is quite likely to be perceived by the researcher as urgent.
4 Researchers will not necessarily label the issue they have as 'research data management', so what they ask and who they ask for help is again unpredictable. An advice service has to be both visible and able to explain clearly the scope of the RDS. Equally it's probable that the service may be asked questions somewhat beyond its remit, which it may seek to answer or refer to others. For example, researchers might well ask about relevant standards or anonymisation techniques.

5 Drawing the line between information and advocacy may also be problematic.

A big part of the advice service will probably be around data management planning. The topic is important enough to have a chapter of its own (Chapter 13).

As in any form of advice service, there are some general principles it makes sense to observe. For example, the American Reference and User Services Association (RUSA, 2013; 2017) identify the following five factors as key to a successful reference service:

1 Visibility/approachability – the service needs to be visible to its potential users and offer an approachable appearance.
2 Interest – in responding to initial enquiries there is a need to project a sense of interest in questions asked.
3 Listening/inquiring – it is widely understood that the presenting issue of the user may not reflect what they really mean to ask. So listening carefully and asking the right questions is key to the interaction.
4 Searching – finding the answer or finding someone who knows the answer is obviously a key process. Signposting to other services or individuals may be as important as finding an answer.
5 Follow up – rather than simply answering a question it is a good practice to seek to follow up: to discover whether the information given was really useful and how it was used, in order to improve responses to future enquiries.

In adapting these principles to the RDM context, there is probably a greater need to stress dialogue and relationship than is common in the reference interview. Since what is being considered is not a factual answer, which can be offered definitively, as is arguably possible with many reference queries, and because the person posing the question is an expert about their topic and the norms of research in their area, it is likely that the transaction will be more of a complex dialogue than a simple reference query.

Making the RDS visible

As a relatively new body of ideas, RDM itself needs explaining. The RDS needs to make itself visible. This can be done in the ways one might expect:

- attending meetings at faculty and departmental level, be that with senior managers or departmentally based research staff
- running special events, e.g. around open access day or to promote re-usable resources
- through a survey of staff about current practices, which helps to draw attention to the existence of services as well as collecting data about current needs (see Chapter 9)
- at staff induction or within wider training events
- through its own website and social media presence
- through a network of local departmental level champions.

An RDS will have its own communication strategy, defining for a number of key audiences specific types of messages, suitable channels and timing. Such audiences are likely to include:

- senior management – major policy shifts and service developments
- departments and individual academics – basic advocacy and practical advice
- other service providers – co-ordination of support.

Embedding information and advice within existing research processes where possible will improve communication because this way information is seen at the point of need, so is likely to be more effective than general broadcast messages without specific contexts.

Ideally the service is responsive and personalised, including individual chats and bespoke advice, but in practical terms the web presence will be important as a reference point for basic information.

Exploring further

Think about the institution you work for or one you know about and make a list of who its key stakeholders are. What do they need to know about RDM? What is the best channel for communicating with them? Are there some predictable times when these messages can or need to be promoted?

Frequently asked questions

It is a very useful way to understand the meaning of RDM to consider 'What will I actually be asked?' The more obvious questions will be things like:

- What is data? What counts as data from the perspective of funders or the institution?
- Where can I find details of funders' requirements?
- What is a data management plan?
- Where should I store my data?
- Where can I share my data?
- When don't I have to share data?
- Isn't sharing data in a paper enough?
- What are the responsibilities of PhD students to share data?

Start preparing an FAQ for your own use; it could ultimately be the basis for your website.

More challenging questions are likely to arise such as:

- How do I make my DMP stand out?
- What are the issues around storing non-digital data?
- How can I anonymise photos or videos?
- What wording should I use in my consent form to allow for data reuse?
- What data should be kept and what should be discarded?
- What are the best formats for data storage? And data preservation?
- What metadata standards are appropriate for describing a particular dataset?
- What is the cost of data storage?
- What licences are suggested for data sharing?

Exploring further

Look at some RDM websites that have already been created by institutions, be that in an institution you have an interest in and its comparators, or looking at different types of institution. Make some notes on:

- content on the home page
- the main types of content in sub-pages/sections
- the structure
- the base URL
- 'branding' of the service or parts of the service such as the data repository
- use of imagery
- tone of text.

Pick some of the best elements from each site to produce a website outline for your idea of the ideal website.

The RDM website

Your review probably revealed rather similar underlying content and structure across the websites, even if the main home page looks different visually. Common elements are:

- an explanation of RDM – including what research data is and is not, couched in terms for researchers of any discipline
- the basics of the case for RDM
- the institutional policy or a summary of key aspects such as:
  - who is responsible for what
  - who does it apply to, e.g. just funded research or student projects led by someone else
  - perhaps a short summary of what individual researchers' responsibilities are
- information about funder policies: rules for applications and end-of-project requirements
- information about DMPs, such as tools to help compose them and examples
- advice on security/active data
- advice on IPR, licensing (including Creative Commons), legal issues such as data protection legislation
- an FAQ
- news of training and other events
- contact details for advice and offers of tailored services
- a link to the institutional repository and related documentation
- guidance on where to search for data sources for re-use
- glossary of terms
- social media presence – some services are actively blogging and on Twitter. This may be more for knowledge sharing with other RDS than with researchers.

Websites vary greatly from very comprehensive approaches to ones that keep things simple and focus on conveying the responsibilities of the researcher in as direct way as possible. A common strategy is to present information structured around the research lifecycle, as a way of helping the reader navigate to the answer they are looking for when they need it.

Of course, the tone of presentation is important. The aim is probably to persuade the user that the topic is important, but not create anxiety. It is important to mirror the wider research culture and the culture in the institution, and to avoid too bureaucratic a tone. Reflecting researchers' own views on the importance of the topic through videos and quotes is more likely to help them engage but if the material is about a very different subject or method they may immediately infer that it is not relevant to them.

Any website is better with imagery, but visualising RDM as a concept is not easy. One is likely to fall back on images of researchers or images of the digital, such as lots of 0s and 1s. It is hard to represent RDM as an issue, but imagery will have a subliminal impact on how readers view the content.

There is a good source of Creative Commons-licensed illustrations of data issues by the Danish graphic artist Jorgen Stamp (see https://digitalbevaring.dk/illustration).

Key challenges for advice and support

If resources were no issue, support could be offered and tailored to each individual researcher. For big projects individual support would be offered. If projects build in some costing for RDM so much the better. Normally, however, there simply are not the staff resources in the RDS to offer this level of service. Rather, website and virtual enquiry services are key to providing information. But it will be a dilemma of whether to provide a comprehensive or more accessible service. Representing RDM visually is hard. Timing is also crucial. Researchers really want just-in-time support, but they have to be aware of the issue and the services available to know when just-in-time is. The foundations of RDM have to be in place early, e.g. at the point of planning data collection, especially where human subjects are involved. Explaining RDM through the lifecycle helps the researcher navigate to relevant material quickly, but different research has very different lifecycles.

References

RUSA (2013) *Guidelines for Behavioral Performance of Reference and Information Service Providers*, American Library Association, www.ala.org/rusa/resources/guidelines/guidelinesbehavioral.

RUSA (2017) *Professional Competencies for Reference and User Services Librarians*, American Library Association, www.ala.org/rusa/resources/guidelines/professional.

CHAPTER 12

Practical data management

Aims

The aim of this chapter is to review the aspects of practical data management that have a bearing on RDM. It will help you think about the day-to-day data management issues researchers face as an important aspect of RDM.

Introduction

The issues dealt with in this chapter can be introduced by the story of the poster that was supposedly once seen in a university computer lab. The poster offered a reward to whoever had stolen a laptop. It did not ask for the return of the laptop or even all the data on it, just the files in a single folder called 'thesis data'. The poster explained that the folder contained the student's only copy of the data for their PhD, and that if it is not recovered the student cannot complete their doctorate. Quite a large reward was offered, but it was negotiable. The student was willing to pay more for the files. The thief was welcome to keep the laptop. No questions would be asked of whoever claimed the reward. We don't know if anyone did claim the reward. Actually we don't know if the whole story is true. It could be. It reflects that if data is core to some research work, the loss of data is a critical area of risk.

Laptops get stolen or lost all the time. They are notoriously unreliable. Surely people know this and back up their data and document the back-ups? Actually, no, the evidence seems to be that people are quite bad about managing their 'stuff', even critical files: they are not necessarily good at managing risk in an intelligent way. Unexpected eventualities such as fires or natural disasters do happen, which can endanger valuable material such as research data. In a rapidly changing technical environment people can be unclear about the changing nature of the risks they are taking with digital material. For example, cloud storage seems like an easy solution to storing a lot of data. But of course there are security issues. The proliferation of cloud storage platforms itself can lead to losing track of data.

Such issues of practical data management are highly relevant to RDM. Researchers are increasingly creating large amounts of digital data. But they have often not learned systematically about how to manage digital content, especially for the long term. Alerting them to the issues could be a key part of motivating them to take RDM seriously. Rather than appealing to their principled belief in open science or the driver of funder mandates, issues of practical data management are immediately relevant to getting to the end of the project. It is important to nearly every researcher that they manage their digital data for their own immediate benefit. You will recall from Chapter 4 that good data housekeeping was actually central to research practice in the case of SoilTrec.

Exploring further

One of the techniques we use when we introduce students to the issues around RDM as a whole is to set them a self-assessment questionnaire which explores their current personal information management practices, i.e. the way they manage their personal files. The aim is to get them thinking about the key issues. Figure 12.1 shows some of the questions we use. You could adapt them for use in your training.

Work through the questions yourself, and reflect on where, if anywhere, you have vulnerabilities in how you yourself manage digital files. What other questions could you add to prompt people to think more about their practical data management practices?

1. How many documents and files (both print and electronic) have you collected/created for your work in the last year?

< 100	100 > 999	1000–4999	5000+

2. What percentage of the collection is digital?

< 25%	25–50%	50–75%	75% >

Figure 12.1 *Questionnaire on personal information practices*

3. What percentage of the digital collection is . . .?

	< 25%	25–50%	50–75%	75% >
Word documents				
Stored on a desktop PC at home				
Stored on a laptop				
Stored on a tablet				
Stored on a phone				
Stored on my university drive				
Stored in the cloud (Dropbox, etc.)				
Stored on a memory disk				
Stored on an external hard-drive				

4. Backing up files

I back up my files	Daily	Weekly	Monthly	Rarely	Never

5. Do you agree or disagree with the following statements?

	Agree	Neutral	Disagree	No opinion
I often have difficulty refinding a document that I created				
I often have difficulty refinding something I found before				
I have lost a version of a document I was working on for my studies				
Finding documents across my different devices is a big problem				
The fact that part of my collection is print and part electronic causes problems				
Sharing documents effectively with others causes problems				
I regularly delete old versions of files and useless information				
I follow a regular convention when creating file names				

6. Passwords – which statement is correct [tick one]?

I use one password for everything	
I have one password for every system and website	
I have one secure password; and for low risk systems use the same password	

Figure 12.1 *Continued*

You may well be very well organised, but most people are not. The questionnaire in Figure 12.1 is designed to reveal this to people by prompting them to think about what they do day to day. What we know from the literature about personal information management as a whole is that:

- We all create and collect a lot of material.
- Managing this is hard because:
  - the material is hybrid between print and digital
  - it is diverse in terms of file types and document types
  - it is fragmented in where it is kept: on our work computer, on our home laptop, on our tablet, on our phone, on our digital camera, in the cloud, on external memory . . .
  - we operate within a complex and rapidly changing infrastructure.
- We do not spend a lot of effort on managing our stuff. We are reluctant to invest valuable time in such housekeeping rather than the 'real' tasks of research, like analysing data. But we do worry about it.
- We do not follow basic advice on things like file naming, backing data up and security.

Of course, in everyday life we probably think the risk is low because the value of the digital material is low. But much of this disorganised and careless way of managing material carries over into our working lives. If research data is critical to research, then we need to be better at managing this material than we are usually with most of our stuff.

Exploring further

Another interesting exercise is to install a characterisation tool such as Windirstat (https://windirstat.net/). Windirstat produces summaries and visualisations of the folder structures and file types and file sizes on a computer drive. It can be quite enlightening about the amount of material you have.

Try talking through with a colleague or friend what material you have and explaining its origins and value. In doing so it will become apparent that someone coming to the material will have a great difficulty understanding it.

You could also play the game of trying to explain to a colleague what files are in a particular folder. This helps in revealing the near-impossibility of a third party understanding what material is and how it is organised.

Another good example to get people thinking is asking them to reflect on their digital photo storage. We take an increasing number of photos, but on multiple devices, using various software to edit it. We rarely bother to properly tag or back up this material. Review how you store your own photos: it is probably quite complex, yet ultimately has a number of flaws.

Risks and risk management
The main risks
Digital material is fragile. A list of the main risks around any digital data would probably include:

- Theft or loss of a device or back-up storage.
- Corruption of back-up material. Even if it is stored securely, the process of digital rot means that files can become illegible over time. Back-ups need to be checked.
- Difficulty locating files or relevant versions of files. Actually doing too many copies of a file, if file-naming conventions are not followed, can lead to inability to find the right version of a file. When people are actively working on data they rely on memory to recall the most up-to-date version. A few months later, trying to work out which version is live can be hard.
- Accidental deletion.
- Colleagues move taking data with them or leaving data without documenting them fully enough.
- Not enough documentation about the context is supplied to understand the data, e.g. what values in a spreadsheet actually are.
- Obsolescence of file types or software.

To researchers their data are critical, but there are some types of material that are particularly high risk, notably:

- files containing personal information, especially prior to any anonymisation process
- unique data that cannot be collected again.

What to tell researchers
In this context researchers would benefit from basic instruction in how to manage their material. The main topics that probably every researcher should know about would be:

- risk management
- file organisation and file naming
- back-ups
- security.

Risk assessment

Not all data, even all research data, is highly valuable or at risk. Where there are vulnerabilities they can be managed. It may be useful to talk to researchers, especially those working in large projects, about basic risk management. This implies thinking systematically about risk assessment, and perhaps introducing the idea of risk logs.

Table 12.1 *The structure of a risk log*

Risk description	A textual description of the risk concerned
Probability	The likelihood of the risk occurring, from low (1) to high (5)
Severity	The impact if the risk did occur, from low to high
Risk score	The probability multiplied by the severity – a measure of the overall risk. Low probability/severity items can be tolerated. Medium probability/severity items need to be treated. Where there is high risk there is probably a need to take more fundamental action.
Timescale	When the risk could occur
Owner	Who is responsible for management of the risk, e.g. the data steward
Action to be taken	Plan to mitigate the risk

A regular, systematic analysis of risks is part of basic project management. It is highly relevant to research data.

File organisation and naming

Certainly in the context of a large project with multiple researchers, establishing a file plan and following some agreed convention on file naming is vital. Some basic file-naming advice is that file names should be:

- consistent
- short and meaningful
- avoid special characters, spaces (use dashes or underscores instead)
- use versioning, again following a convention
- follow a date convention: YYYYMMDD is often preferred.

Back-ups of active data

Some researchers only have small amounts of data, and this can be stored within a standard allocation of file space on institutional servers. This means that it is backed up. However, even a few photo, audio or video files (depending on format) can fill up disk space very quickly. In this case the researcher needs to make more effort to ensure data is backed up. A few basic principles of backing material up are:

* LOCKSS – lots of copies make stuff safe
* 3:2:1 rule – ideally one should have three back-ups, on two types of media and with at least one off site. This protects the researcher against issues with both the media
* cloud storage is fantastic because it allows you to access data from multiple locations. However, it is not without its risks, in terms of potential security breaches or risk of unexpected downtime. Because laws vary internationally there may be problems arising from material being held in a different jurisdiction.

Promoting practical data management

Simply introducing examples of worrying cases of data loss to researchers is not likely to improve data management in itself (or make you popular). Emphasis should be given to encouraging researchers to develop data management plans based on good principles and that are kept up on an ongoing basis as the project proceeds. Yet the appeal to the researcher's own vested interests in being confident that they will have access to their data and be able to find material in the future is likely to be a core part of your strategy for promoting RDM.

Exploring further

Disciplinary practices in managing data vary widely. Some fields like some health research including randomised control trials are governed by very well developed data quality and integrity standards. This is driven by their use of sensitive and personal data.

It is worth trying to find out more about what current conventions, if any, there are in an area of research of interest to you.

Further reading

There are two good books on data management, the first directed more at scientists; the other primarily for social scientists.

Briney, K. (2015) *Data Management for Researchers: Organize, maintain and share your data for research success*, Pelagic Publishing Ltd.

Corti, L., Van den Eynden, V., Bishop, L. and Woollard, M. (2014) *Managing and Sharing Research Data: A guide to good practice*, Sage.

Mantra (http://mantra.edina.ac.uk) is a fantastic self-directed learning package which deals with many aspects of RDM, such as data storage, data handling, etc.

CHAPTER 13

Data management planning

Aims

The aim of the chapter is to explain data management planning and to explore how best to support it.

The data management plan

Increasingly funders are requiring that any proposal for a project must include a detailed explanation of how research data will be managed during the project, including such aspects as how much data will be collected, in which formats, how participant confidentiality will be protected and which parts of the data will be shared at project close. This is often called a data management plan (DMP), though different funders give it different names.

The requirement to write a DMP may be one of the first times a researcher may encounter the idea of RDM. For many researchers this requirement may feel like an unwelcome extra hurdle in the long and arduous task of writing a research proposal. It is unclear if a bad DMP will really affect the likelihood of being funded. Because it deals with seemingly minute aspects of data management it may not feel very important, in the context of the wider ambitions of a project – although, as we saw in Chapter 4, data management could also be recognised as a cornerstone of a successful project. A researcher may well feel it is almost impossible to anticipate exactly how much data they might have in megabytes or what preservation formats they might choose. They are likely to see it as quite a technical document that needs input from the computing service, around what data storage facilities exist. But they are quite likely also to be unclear about what the funder is really looking for in writing such a document.

Because of the detail and unfamiliarity of the DMP, having to write one frequently leads researchers, right at the last minute before a proposal submission deadline, to seek help from the RDS. It will probably be one of the main enquiries from staff that the RDS receives. Working out how best to support researchers to write their DMP is a key task for the RDS. It is also a critical opportunity for the RDS, because it is one of the main occasions that researchers might actively seek help.

At a deeper level the DMP has great potential as the vehicle for creating a good RDM culture. Plans that exist before projects even begin can greatly improve RDM, so long as they are:

- used to guide action in the project, rather than being just filed away
- updated as the project unfolds
- informed by good practice.

An organisation in which all research projects had a DMP would be highly likely to be an exemplar for RDM. Creating a DMP culture would underwrite a strong RDM culture.

The benefits of DMPs
There is a strong case for data management planning. It is all about thinking ahead. What data will the research need and how will the researchers obtain these? How are they going to document the data and where will they store them safely and securely whilst they are working with them? And when the project draws to a close, which of these data need to be kept and possibly even shared with the wider community, and how can that be achieved? The dividend is that the researcher is well organised from the moment the project actually kicks off.

Thinking ahead about what will happen to the data in a research project helps to decide how careful the research staff should be with documenting their data. Planning data management will therefore help to ensure that data remains accessible and comprehensible in the near, middle and distant future so that the data creator, as well as all other researchers with whom the data are shared, can find them and understand them.

But planning also helps to be prepared for data preservation and sharing in other ways, because decisions made at the start of a project will influence what the researcher is able to do with the data later on. For example, if they obtained informed consent from participants that mentions data sharing it will be much easier to share data at the end of the project. Trying to change this retrospectively would be much harder. Ownership of data in collaborations and partnerships may restrict what you can and cannot do with the data later on: so understanding these from the start of the project is important.

There are other benefits too. Planning storage and backing up helps to avoid the risk of data loss and unauthorised access. And if the work will be carried out by a project team, it is essential – as we have seen from the case study in Chapter 4 – to provide guidelines for everyone in the team to establish clarity early on about who is responsible for what, so that essential tasks do not fall between the cracks. It also ensures continuity if project staff leave or new researchers join. It will also help to establish what resources are required for data management, such as staff time for creating metadata, or storage requirements for large amounts of data such as high-definition videos or automatically captured field measurements. A DMP will help identify if extra resources are required from the funder, too. Again, asking for money retrospectively is unlikely to work.

Finally, a plan will help a research project to meet legal and ethical requirements, such as those relating to informed consent from participants, as well as requirements from funders and publishers. Indeed, an increasing number of public funders and charities are requiring data management plans when applying for funding, and even when funders do not ask for a formal plan, they may still have expectations regarding the management of live data, the long-term preservation of archived data and data sharing. An increasing number of publishers are also requiring that data under-pinning a publication should be publicly accessible, often as a supplement with the publication or via a public repository where the data can be identified with a unique DOI. Publishers of academic peer-reviewed journals, such as Elsevier and Springer Nature, have developed research data policies for their journals, making data sharing compulsory for some Springer Nature journals at the time of writing. Other publishers are following suit.

The content of a DMP
According to the Digital Curation Centre's (2013) authoritative checklist for data management planning, the following topics are likely areas that need to be covered:

1 administrative data

2 data collection
3 documentation and metadata
4 ethics and legal compliance
5 storage and back-up
6 selection and preservation
7 data sharing
8 responsibilities and resources.

These topics follow the research lifecycle, with compliance and responsibilities at the centre of the circle as of relevance through the whole process.

Administrative data is simply basic data such as a project title, the name of the lead researcher and the dates when the project ran.

A research project often begins with the collection of data (2), either by finding existing data sources that might be re-used or by creating new data that help to answer the central research questions of the project. Whilst these data are created, researchers need to ensure that the collection methods are properly documented, and that the data themselves – whether they are recordings of interviews, text passages, numbers in spreadsheets, images or film materials – have sufficient metadata attached to them so that others understand how the data were created and make sense of them (3).

Particularly with research that involves human subjects there will be a need to do so ethically, so the plan must abide by institutional or professional guidelines on ethical matters and with laws such as those around data protection (4).

Subsequently, the documented data will need to be stored securely and backed up regularly, in order to avoid data loss or unauthorised access to personal or commercially sensitive information (5).

Towards the end of the project, a selection will need to be made of data that needs to be preserved, for example to serve as the underlying evidence of published papers and other research outputs, or as a dataset in its own right. These data then will need to find a permanent home, either in an institutional repository or in an external data centre (6).

Decisions need to be made about whether the data can be shared, whether any access restrictions should apply, and how this is achieved: where will the data be preserved and how will access be restricted? Does the funder require the use of a particular provider? Where will the data find their maximum use? Will they be shared via an institutional repository, or a cloud-based service such as Figshare or Zenodo? And are there any costs involved which need to be planned for? (7).

It makes sense to determine who is responsible for data as a whole (perhaps the principal investigator) as well as defining the responsibilities of individuals involved in the project, e.g. what should those collecting data do about storing and documenting data as they go (8).

Planning data management and data sharing is something that is best done with others, especially in larger and more complicated research projects. This may involve the research staff who are actually collecting, processing and analysing the data, as they will have insight in the needs for and possibilities of data storage giving access to the live data, and the documentation of the data. But it could also include laboratory or technical staff, professional services staff (such as IT services who may be able to assist with data storage and security, and library services who may advise on data management planning and metadata) and even external data centres where the data will be hosted once the project is finished, but who may be able to help organise and document the data as per their requirements.

Exploring further
Funders have different requirements for data management plans (DMPs), but they are likely to cover the areas defined above in some form. This will make a lot more sense to you if you find and read one or two. An example is quoted in the next section.

Reading an example DMP
A good example of a data management plan is written by Bren Neale, Professor of Life Course and Family Research at the University of Leeds. Her DMP for a sociological, qualitative longitudinal study examining the lived experiences and support needs of young fathers can be found on the RDMRose website (Neale, n.d.).

Neale begins by saying that the data management plan will be kept under review as the research progresses, and she finished with the promise that she 'will review our data management plan at regular intervals – it will be a standing item on the agenda of our project meetings.'

The plan then first assesses the data that will be used. She evaluates whether there are any existing datasets that can be used to answer the central questions of her research, and then continues to provide information on the new data that will need to be created. In particular she mentions audio files and transcripts of interviews and focus groups, and visual materials such as timelines and photographic records. These will be collected in open formats such as Word files and MP3 audio files. File formats that are open-source and well documented ensure the longevity of the data. So does quality assurance of the data, which is the next topic Neale discusses: the data will be checked thoroughly so that they are archive-ready. She proposes to use a template that she calls a data 'roadmap' which is a chart that logs 'the data trail for each case from generation in the field through to deposit in the archive':

> Facilitating re-use by others as well as aiding longitudinal analysis by the primary teams requires detailed documentation of the data, which is organised in two dimensions – case by case and wave by wave. . . . The metadata includes: guide to the aims and objectives of the project, including research questions; fieldwork materials, interview documents, letter and information leaflets, research diaries and field notes; keywords assigned to data files and transcripts to denote content and aid data discovery. We will also consider the viability of incorporating thematic coding files (generated through NVivo Framework) and other descriptive files (e.g. pen portraits of participants) within our dataset.

Other topics Neale covers are the storage and backing-up procedures and that all files will be 'well labelled and logically organised' with 'robust procedures for version control'. Finally, she discusses how responsibilities for research data management will be divided in the project team, and whether there are any restrictions on data sharing, including issues relating to intellectual property rights and informed consent:

> Ethical considerations are of vital importance to the research and underpin our data management plan. Consent forms will include consent for archiving. To ensure consent is properly informed our information leaflets for participants will include archiving details and potential re-use. We do not envisage any difficulty with this: evidence from our current research and that of others indicates that participants are positive about the preservation of their accounts for archiving and re-use.

Exploring further

Do some searches to try and find some other examples of DMPs:

- Funders often supply a few examples.
- Some support organisations collect examples where they can, e.g. DCC do so.
- The *Research Ideas and Outcomes* journal (https://riojournal.com) publishes all types of outputs from the entire research cycle, including DMPs.
- You may have access to ones that have been written at your own institution, if you are working in an RDS.

Having put together a small collection, try analysing them using the eight-point checklist outlined previously.

- How do you think the DMPs could be improved?
- Do you think the examples you have are specific enough?

Give some thought to who might need to be consulted to provide the best possible DMP.

Common pitfalls

From our experience of supporting data management planning, a few common pitfalls are:

- failing to look for existing datasets that can be re-used to answer the project research questions
- failing to fully assess where to keep data securely and safely for the duration of the project – there are often issues around personal information, cloud storage and data encryption while collecting sensitive information in the field
- a lack of understanding of what metadata and documentation are needed
- difficulty assessing what data to keep for long-term preservation, often with a reluctance to discard anything at all
- uncertainty about where and how to share data – licences can be particularly challenging.

Supporting data management planning

Probably one of the most important functions of the RDS is to support data management planning. Support can be offered in a number of ways.

There are many tools and templates that can help researchers writing a data management plan. They come as checklists and templates and can be in the form of a digital file (Word, PDF) or an online tool. There are templates for doctoral projects and templates that meet the requirements of a specific funder. Many institutions have a DMP template that fits the institutional context, although these are often based on the checklist from the DCC:

- DMPOnline in the UK, http://dmponline.ac.uk
- DMPTool in the USA, http://dmptool.org
- DMP Assistant in Canada, https://portagenetwork.ca.

DMPOnline, for example, presents a list of questions based on the funder of the project. Institutions can also add institution-specific templates and institution specific guidance, and it is possible to add plans for different stages of a project, e.g. for a grant application and a fuller plan after the grant has been awarded.

You could design templates or boilerplate text for data management plans that fit the research undertaken at the institution and target different groups of researchers; it could be useful to have a different template for doctoral research projects.

You might provide workshops and training sessions. The drawback of this approach is that researchers may feel they are too busy to attend such sessions, and do not really recognise they need the training until the moment they suddenly need to be able to write a DMP for a particular proposal. Compared to the challenges of writing the main part of a proposal, it may not feel important enough.

Providing a DMP read-through service is often one of the most popular data management services at universities. While the services mentioned above are useful, as each project is unique, researchers need tailored support. It is vital for the service to have a good knowledge of funder requirements and to check against a funder's reviewer guidance or other guidelines if they exist. It is probable that a response needs to be rather rapid, as funders are working to application deadlines.

Embedding data management planning into the research process, for example, mandating data management plans as part of ethical approval, or as part of progression reporting for doctoral students, is a way to spread the DMP writing culture throughout the body of researchers.

Exploring further
Look at the requirements for one or two key research funders. Do they ask for something equivalent to a DMP? What is it called? What elements are required? Thinking about some of these elements, how would you go about finding an answer to them?

Further reading
The following study was based on a study of a collection of DMPs as a way of studying patterns in intentions to share data, etc.:

Parham, S. W., Carlson, J., Hswe, P., Westra, B. and Whitmire, A. (2016) Using Data Management Plans to Explore Variability in Research Data Management Practices Across Domains, *International Journal of Digital Curation*, **11** (1), 53–67.

References
Digital Curation Centre (2013) Checklist for a Data Management Plan, www.dcc.ac.uk/sites/default/files/documents/resource/DMP/DMP_Checklist_2013.pdf.

Neale, B. (n.d.) *Following Young Fathers: Data management plan*, http://rdmrose.group.shef.ac.uk/wp-content/uploads/Resource-7-1-Soc-Document05-RDMRose.docx.

CHAPTER 14

Advocacy for data management and sharing

Aims

The aim of this chapter is to prompt you to think about strategies to influence researchers to see the importance of RDM to themselves.

Introduction

Many international and national bodies governing research have expressed their commitment to the ideal of open data. For all the qualifications, this is the ideal put forward by the UK *Concordat on Open Research Data* discussed in Chapter 5, for example. Yet data could be shared in a number of ways, many of which may be more familiar to researchers than open unrestricted sharing in a data repository, for example:

- with collaborators in a research group
- with collaborators beyond the institution in a particular project
- by request with peers
- within a particular community of researchers
- as supplementary information or otherwise linked to a publication.

There are some compelling reasons why most research data could be potentially shared in these different ways and much of it openly. This section considers some of those reasons.

You will recall from Chapter 4 that the soil scientist professor Steve Banwart said a lot about sharing within a specific project. Other RDMRose interviewees talked about data sharing:

Richard Rowe is a senior lecturer in the Department of Psychology at the University of Sheffield.

> As a researcher, in some ways, it feels a bit strange to collect data and then just have anyone analyse it, but I think, as far as I understand it, there's ample

time to do the analyses that you promised to do before everyone else gets hold of it. And as I say, a lot of the data that I work with is publicly available, so that's sort of always there for anybody to look at. That causes some problems in that you can end up with the same people doing the same work and duplicating efforts. The worst case of this I know of is one that I was involved in. [He describes the setting up of a project to reanalyse an existing dataset]. Then three weeks before we started, we just happened to turn on the news and see that someone had reported and done exactly the same analyses, and it was on the news, with exactly the same dataset. [Fortunately the funder allowed them to do another piece of work.] If we'd found out three weeks before the end of the project, when we'd nearly finished, then that could have wasted an enormous amount of money and an enormous amount of time. I mean, I think some of the studies try to keep a record of who's downloading the data and what they're going to do with it, but it's just so hard. . . . My experience of working with publicly available datasets is that there isn't an awful lot of checking of results going around. To replicate an analysis could be done, but it would be an enormous amount of work to get to the point of doing that, in terms of preparing the data in the same way that the original group did. So I've never really heard of anyone doing that, but the potential for it to be there is a good thing. I don't think that's a particular problem.

Bernard Corfe is a senior lecturer at the Department of Oncology at the University of Sheffield.

I think open data is really important. So a lot of my work is in the area of bioinformatics, and that is extremely driven by open data, and also open source. But the argument in bioinformatics is that it's not necessarily the person who generates the data who is the best person to analyse it, and also that there is more to be gained from merging datasets and analysing much larger datasets than there is from one person working on a dataset. So I think from those bioinformatics principles, I can see those applying to all sorts of areas of science, that if you can generate datasets in such a way that they can be merged, you've got a much more powerful way of analysing work. And also, a better way of seeing why one group get one result and another group might get a completely opposing result. If you can share that data and see the underlying differences, be it different age groups of the populations, or different socioeconomic groups, or different genetics, or whatever, it gives us better understanding. And then that is in itself informative. If you can see why two studies end up with different outcomes, then you can see why you might reach through to personalised medicine or personalised healthcare. So I think there are enormous amounts to be gained by open data, but I think tied into that is an absolute need for data reporting standards. So proper use of conserved vocabularies, proper structuring and organisation of data, rather than just chucking your spreadsheets into the ether. So that works really well for people who are working on metabolomics or proteomics. But actually if we can generate reporting standards for work in nutrition, or work in sociology or whatever, and generate datasets that can be merged, then, you know, the future looks very very bright, I think. My argument is, there's no point in having open data without standards . . . without really tight standards. So areas like proteomics, microarray and genomics are absolutely fantastic. They're kind of leaders in reporting standards. Other areas that I work in, in nutrition, are, you know, back in the 1950s, and absolutely terrible. They don't share, they don't have their own reporting standards, they have no repositories. And so, I can see from the part of me that stands in the bioinformatics world the potential, and the part of me that stands in the nutrition world of what a mountain to climb there is in some disciplines. It's fairly simple. It needs to come down from top journals saying you can't publish unless you've got a repository, but in that case you need a repository, in that case you need structured vocabularies. So there are steps, a good few, you know, not too many.

Exploring further
Refresh your memory about what Professor Banwart said in the interview extracts in Chapter 4, and also read what Richard Rowe and Bernard Corfe thought. What seem to be the main drivers and barriers for sharing data here?

Drivers for data sharing
In fact, the arguments for data sharing and for RDM more generally are complex and multi-layered.

In terms of the direct benefits to research:

1   If data is shared, more research can be published using it, e.g. by asking totally new research questions or through it being combined with other sources.

In terms of research visibility:

2   The researcher should be cited for the data use and such data citations are likely to increase the citation of their publications too. So it increases research visibility.

3 Data sharing could be a starting point for a collaboration.

In terms of the benefits to research integrity:

4 The findings can be reproduced by other researchers, so ensuring research integrity.

In terms of compliance:

5 If the public funded the work, e.g. directly through government grants, there is an obligation to make the best use of the data.
6 Many funders of research require data sharing. Researchers want funds, so they will need to do it.
7 Many institutions expect it. The RDS itself exists to promote this recognition.
8 Many major journals are now requiring it as a condition for publication.

In addition, in terms of research efficiency, there are other arguments that would make RDM relevant to most researchers, even if no data sharing was imagined at all:

9 Researchers may want to share data effectively and securely with colleagues in a research team.
10 They will want reliable access themselves to the data during the lifetime of a project and beyond.

Exploring further

All this sounds pretty compelling. But the truth is that many researchers are not actually sharing their data. How can that be? Give some thought to the problems researchers might have with the notion of sharing data, and with the concept of 'open data' in particular. What counter-arguments can you think of?

What should researchers do to promote data use and re-use?

White et al. (2013) make what they call nine simple suggestions for making it easier to use and re-use data, in the context of ecology and evolutionary biology:

1 share it
2 provide metadata
3 provide raw, unprocessed data
4 present the data according to standards, e.g. in standard file formats, using standards within tables
5 use good null values, in other words follow a good convention about differences between missing data and where the data filed should actually say zero and how to represent such values – they suggest the best option is leave blanks
6 make it easy to combine the data with other data, e.g. by providing contextual data
7 have quality control
8 use a widely used repository
9 share the data using a well-established and open licence, thus giving people the opportunity to use it in different ways.

The suggestions are a good starting point for describing what is needed to share data, albeit they are assuming the data is quantitative. These may indeed be simple suggestions for their field, but there are a number of questions that are not trivial to answer:

• Where is the best place to share data? What if there is not a widely used repository in the field?
• What exactly are the metadata or contextual data needed to understand the data?
• What standards for describing data are there?
• What data licences are there and which might be appropriate?

These four questions begin to open up the practical issues around data sharing. But the barriers are not merely technical.

Panda talk

Many people who work in RDM use the video 'Data Sharing and Management Snafu in 3 Short Acts' in their teaching about RDM. It's an amusing six-minute cartoon in which a panda (supposedly an oncologist) tries to persuade a teddy bear to share his data. The teddy bear just about manages to give every possible excuse you can imagine for not handing over his data:

- He repeatedly says that the data is in the published paper, when the panda really wants the raw data to do a different type of analysis.
- He only has one copy of it and it is on a memory stick in a box somewhere which he cannot find because he is moving house.
- The software to read the data is no longer available.
- He does not recall the meaning of the data labels.
- The person who knows the meaning of the data labels has left the organisation and is effectively untraceable.

It is obvious that the teddy bear just does not want to share his data, even though his funding and place of publication requires it. In a humorous form it brings home some of the frustrations of trying to gain access to another researcher's data. The panda is heroically persistent but ultimately fails to gain useful access. The video is a good starting point for discussing with researchers the issues around RDM.

As he is presented in the video it is hard to feel sympathy for this teddy bear, but if we want to influence real researchers to share their data, we have to take seriously their qualms about data sharing, and work out what will persuade them to share their data or at least manage them effectively. There are actually a lot of reasons, good and bad, that might inhibit a researcher from sharing their data:

1   They invested a lot of time in creating the data and therefore they feel they own it and want to control it.
2   They are worried that someone else will scoop them and analyse their data and publish results from it before they can.
3   They have a vague plan to re-use it in the future.
4   They have concerns that weaknesses in their methodology (real or imagined) might be exposed.
5   They are doubtful that someone who was not involved in the data collection could really understand the data or re-use it in a methodologically valid way.
6   It is extra and unfunded effort to publish data because it means processing and documenting it. Tenopir et al. (2011), in their widely

cited study of researchers' attitude to data sharing, found lack of time and funding to be the most commonly cited reasons for not sharing data.

7   They may simply not have the knowledge and skills to share the data: e.g. they are unaware of appropriate places or whether such repositories would be interested in their data.

8   They may be put off by the 'bureaucracy' around depositing data.

9   They have never re-used data themselves and have not read any work that was based on re-used data. This particular research community may have quite a limited culture of data sharing.

10   They do not have consent from human participants for the data to be re-used.

11   They might be concerned about the confidentiality of participants in their study. In particular, they may have concerns about the way data from different sources can be linked together to identify individuals even in anonymised data.

12   There could be commercial interests that prevent data sharing or issues around client confidentiality.

13   They might be worried about the commercial use of data, or unethical uses by other researchers, or the way one particular researcher might pass on the data to others.

14   They might be unsure about data ownership, e.g. if the university claims it owns research data.

15   They are simply too busy to respond to this query.

16   They are unclear how they are going to be credited or otherwise benefit from sharing their data.

17   What and when are data is itself unclear.

Reflecting on this list of concerns we may begin to have an appreciation for the dilemma of the teddy bear in the video! There are answers in many cases to these issues, but one of the more challenging tasks of the RDM team is to begin to address them.

Exploring further
Start thinking about some of the motives for not sharing data (summarised in the previous section). What are the counter-arguments? What can be done to reassure people with these different qualms?

Some responses

Here are some possible responses to each of the concerns listed previously:

1   The researcher's feeling that they have the right to control the data because of their intellectual effort in creating it has to be respected. Of course, if their research was funded then the funder may still have made it a condition of funding that they manage the data in a particular type of way. Even if it was based on personal research it has to be recognised that this was effectively supported by the institution. But it may be more persuasive to emphasise to them how they can protect their investment and increase its yield by sharing it, than to focus on the obligation to do so.

2   A concern about being scooped is not an unreasonable fear. However, embargo periods can allow a period before data is made available to other researchers. Data sharing is rarely simply open to the world; restrictions can be placed that give the researcher time to make the most of their data.

3   If the researcher has a plan to re-use data in the future, however vague, they may be inhibited from sharing it. They may be thinking of the potential to do a repeat study in a few years. If they share the data now, someone else could do it first. Embargo periods may again be relevant to protecting against this possibility. Talking about the benefits to their own research visibility of sharing the data may also be persuasive.

4   If their concern is about weaknesses in their approach to data analysis, this is a hard concern to address. It is one that is unlikely to be openly articulated, making it even harder to tackle. It does seem to be a concern, particularly with younger researchers. Whether the fear is justified or not, they are seeking to protect their own credibility and reputation. Nevertheless, good research practice, even outside subjects where replicability is a common practice, implies honesty and transparency.

5   Methodological concerns about whether another researcher could use the data if they were not involved in its collection is a potentially valid feeling that must be respected. It is a common argument used by qualitative researchers, because of their sense of the unique understanding built up with participants during data collection. But documenting the data is also part of good practice.

For example, field notes that accompany interviews can help a future researcher make sense of the data. Ultimately, there may be cases where not enough of the context can really be made explicit for future researchers to effectively re-use the data. Yet we can point to many examples of data re-use with qualitative data.

6 Preparing data to be shared can be time-consuming, so a researcher's concern that they do not have time to do this is not groundless. Preparing data for sharing involves processing it, choosing what should be kept and thorough documentation. This does have a cost. Hopefully an institutional RDS will support some of the effort. In some cases funders will allot funds to support this activity, if the request is made in the original proposal. Of course this means anticipating the cost a long time before it is incurred. Otherwise, a researcher might be persuaded to see the benefit of the effort through arguments of principle or the citation benefit of sharing the data.

7 It is not unreasonable to say that a researcher may not know how or where to share data. The institutional support services should offer training and advice on this, tailored by discipline. Again, maybe the first step in overcoming this concern is for them to be encouraged to re-use data themselves, in which case they will already have looked across a number of research data repositories and begun to understand how they work.

8 Some 'bureaucracy' around data sharing such as ensuring that basic metadata and documentation is created is inevitable. The sense of this being bureaucracy might be reduced by fitting systems into natural research workflows. It can also be reduced by the RDS taking on some of the burden, for example by supplying some types of metadata or by taking some deposit activities out of their hands.

9 If researchers have no culture of re-use of data they are likely to see requests to share their data as unreasonable or unexpected. That is why the RDS emphasis on promoting existing data sources to researchers may be a promising approach to stimulating data sharing, because it will appeal to researchers to be among the first to benefit from getting good publications without the effort of creating data. Then they may feel happy about reciprocating and sharing their own data. However, if the whole culture of data sharing across the academic community is weak, it will be hard to kick-start sharing at

an institutional level. This sort of challenge is articulated clearly in the interview extract from Professor Corfe.

10 If existing consent forms do not mention data sharing, researchers can probably go back to ethics committees and then to participants to request permission for data to be shared on some basis. Clearly it is much more efficient if this has been thought through before ethics clearance, i.e. towards the beginning of the project. That is why the message about RDM has to be got across to researchers before they collect data, e.g. at the point of creating a data management plan. Integrating RDM training with research ethics (which researchers recognise as important) could pay off here.

11 There are genuine concerns around anonymisation of human data. Big data techniques combining multiple sources of apparently anonymous data can identify individuals. The RDS can help by pointing at resources which explain effective anonymisation techniques.

12 There are also genuine commercial interests that prevent data sharing. These are recognised by most funders. Ultimately, if key relationships with commercial collaborators could be jeopardised researchers are unlikely to take a risk on trying to persuade them to share data. They may well feel as frustrated by the impact of confidentiality on the visibility of their research as you.

13 If a researcher is worried about the commercial use of data or unethical uses by other researchers or the way one particular researcher might pass on the data to others, these can all be addressed in the terms on which data is made available for re-use.

14 Researchers may be unsure about data ownership, but it may be possible for the RDS to give them help in understanding this.

15 The plea by the researcher that they are too busy to do anything about RDM links back to resourcing. Encouraging researchers to account for this work in their data management plan as part of a project proposal could be effective.

16 It is essential that if data is re-used, credit is given to the collector of the data. Talking about data citation practices reassures those sharing data. That is also why a lot of time is invested in creating an infrastructure for data citation that is equivalent to that for citing published resources (see Chapter 5). However, citation is only part of the story. If data sharing is not recognised by institutions in

reward and tenure schemes the incentives for it remain indirect.

17 A more conceptual issue is that it is not necessarily easy to identify 'the data' to be shared. As we discussed in Chapter 3, data is not necessarily an object that can be pointed at. It can appear in multiple versions and usually shared data is some part of a whole dataset. Nevertheless, this is not really a reason not to share data.

Reflecting on these answers it is clear that it is important to differentiate a message about the benefits of open data, the benefits of more restricted forms of data sharing, and the immediate benefits to the researcher of RDM, even where data is not shared. It also becomes clear that the message has to be got across early in the research for it to be most effective e.g. so that funding for processing can be built into a proposal and any ethics application can take it into account. Other recurrent themes seem to be around encouraging researchers to re-use data themselves as a way of changing their attitudes. Simple compliance arguments do not seem the best starting point for a discussion!

Changing the culture

Advocacy is a long-term process. Given the numbers of researchers in any one institution, their entrenched habits of doing research, the range of other demands on them and the limited resources of the RDS, change is not going to be achieved overnight. Gradually changing the culture will be the aim; success hard to measure. But some critical points could be:

- evidence of success stories in finding and re-using existing data to speed up research
- successful cases where a researcher has shared their own data and it has impacted their reputation and citation count on their publications
- evidence that comparator institutions are moving ahead.

Exploring further

As a way of thinking about how to adapt arguments that work with particular groups, consider the following short profiles. How do you think the character views open data and RDM in general? Which of the arguments set out above would they find most compelling? You might want to try a role play with a colleague to work through some of these ideas! Of course, how you might approach the conversation could be influenced by the seniority of the academic as well as their apparent position.

You are an experimental psychologist. You believe passionately that it's vital that data is shared to ensure replication of research. If you don't share data it's basically bad research.

You are an astronomer. Your collaborative projects generate terabytes of data. Open access data and publishing is second nature.

You are a social geographer. You re-use some government data, but you think the long interviews you do in your research are too sensitive.

You are a professor of English. You see digital humanities as an anathema. You would never use the term 'data' for the literary texts you analyse in your research.

You are a computer scientist who regularly works with demanding industry partners. You have an interest in the commercial aspects of your work.

You are a medical researcher doing clinical trials. You have vast experience of secure use of personal information.

Further reading

A seminal work exploring the way that researchers share, or rather fail to share, data – a key context for advocacy – is by Christine Borgman:

Borgman, C. L. (2012) The Conundrum of Sharing Research Data, *Journal of the Association for Information Science and Technology*, **63** (6), 1059–78.

Another seminal work asks the question whether data sharing has an impact on citation:

Piwowar, H. A., Day, R. S. and Fridsma, D. B. (2007) Sharing Detailed Research Data is Associated with Increased Citation Rate, *PLOS ONE*, **2** (3), e308.

Looking at citations of these works will give you a sense of how scholarship around these two key questions is developing.

References

Tenopir, C., Allard, S., Douglass, K., Aydinoglu, A. U., Wu, L., Read, E., Manoff, M. and Frame, M. (2011) Data Sharing by Scientists: Practices and perceptions, *PLOS ONE*, **6** (6), e21101.

White, E. P., Baldridge, E., Brym, Z. T., Locey, K. J., McGlinn, D. J. and Supp, S. R. (2013) Nine Simple Ways to Make it Easier to (Re) Use Your Data,

Ideas in Ecology and Evolution, **6** (2), https://ojs.library.queensu.ca/index.php/IEE/article/view/4608.

CHAPTER 15

Training researchers and data literacy

Aims

The aim of this chapter is to work through the decisions that need to be made to set up a programme of training about research data management.

Introduction

Central to any RDS will be the function of training members of the organisation in RDM. The chapter is organised around a series of inter-related decisions involved in designing such a training programme.

One of the outcomes of your talking to researchers and your more systematic user requirements gathering (Chapter 9) will be to have a feel for what the needs are around the institution. But determining audiences, content and channels for training is in itself quite challenging.

> **Exploring further**
> Think about some of the more engaging CPD or training courses you have been on. What made the best events stand out? It could be:
>
> - the immediate usefulness of what you learned
> - the hands-on time
> - what you learned from other people on the course, as opposed to the trainers
> - the time you were given to talk through how the challenge affected you
> - the warmth and helpfulness of the trainers
> - something else.
>
> Think about how you can manage the learning situation to recreate such a good learning experience for anyone who comes on one of your courses.

Step 1: Who is the training for?

At some level it may be that every researcher in the institution needs some training in basic awareness of institutional policy and guidelines and to draw attention to critical areas of risk. But attempting to develop training that feels relevant to everyone, in every discipline and level of experience, is challenging.

It is probable that people in different meta-disciplines will have widely differing views on what RDM is about. That does not mean that they should be taught separately but it will take extra effort to ensure that the material feels relevant to everyone. An obvious compromise is to organise training by meta-discipline (e.g. for humanities scholars separate from engineers). Training customised to each department or subject discipline may not be scalable.

Actually it could be argued that those with similar methodologies might be best brought together, regardless of their field. Data collection and analysis methods might have more impact on similarity of experience than actual topic of study. Thus quantitative researchers doing survey work, regardless of their subject field, are likely to encounter similar issues around identifying secondary data sources for re-use and data quality.

There is also an issue around seniority. Training research leaders would be ideal. They have the power and responsibility to manage data in funded projects. They can influence others. Given that they are orientated towards gaining funding, they should be concerned with funder policies. But of course they are busy, and are not necessarily very open to new influences. It may make sense to focus on 'early career researchers' and PhD students: they have a bit more time to attend training; they are more open to new ideas, if only because they are not so settled in routine ways of doing things. They are more likely to follow institutional directives than senior researchers, who are a bit more invested in research communities, with their locus outside the institution. Perhaps they are more idealistic and interested in debates around open science. They could well be using more advanced, digital techniques anyway. If one can influence the younger researchers, in the long term the underlying culture around RDM can be changed. But it will take time.

Master's students, and increasingly undergraduates, can be involved in research in their taught programmes. RDM may well be highly relevant to them, if their final projects involve data collection.

Finally, it is worth emphasising that another key group for training would be those supporting research, be that research administrators, librarians or computing staff, whether those in a centralised service or, perhaps even more importantly, those distributed around academic departments.

Step 2: What topics need to be covered?

There have been various attempts to define a curriculum for data literacy (or data information literacy, as some librarians have called it). The following list suggests some of the main areas where training might be offered:

1 critical perspectives on the nature of research data
2 funder requirements
3 writing a DMP; maintaining DMP as an active tool
4 management of active data in a project, including security
5 ethics of data collection, use and re-use
6 legal aspects
7 managing sensitive data
8 data licensing
9 data quality and standards
10 data processing and manipulation
11 database design
12 data analysis – tools and techniques
13 data visualisation – tools and techniques
14 documenting data/metadata
15 searching for secondary data
16 data sharing
17 long-term data preservation
18 citation of data (and software).

Some of these are quite pragmatically oriented to funding (e.g. funder requirements) others are much more technical and could sit in research methods training (e.g. data analysis and visualisation). Those which imply acquisition of immediate skills such as database design and data analysis will be attractive for those building skills.

It is probable that most of the immediate demand for training would come from those seeking support in writing grant applications, and so interested in funder requirements and wanting help with their data management plans.

A more long-term approach would be to stimulate demand for data sharing, by increasing understanding of the benefits and issues of data re-use. But training on finding and re-using data may not generate the same immediate interest and it may be difficult for RDS to facilitate this training because it requires subject knowledge to support adequately.

Exploring further
Examining the 18 areas for data literacy, what do you think would be the main content under each heading? Do you think there are aspects that are missing from the list?

If you are working in a particular institution, which are the priority? Which do you regard as essential for all to know?

Step 3: Who should deliver the training?

Institutions are organised in very different ways, but thinking about fairly typical institutional structures, the training described in Step 2 could be delivered by the library, research administration, archive and records service, computing service, continuing professional development provision, or via academics who teach research methods.

For example, searching for secondary data is akin to doing a literature search, so very naturally would seem to fall in the remit of the library. Management of active data could be seen as something a computing service would deliver. And a course on funders' requirements would seem to fit naturally under the aegis of research administration. Data analysis as such could be part of research methods training, though guidance on tools for data analysis might well sit elsewhere. Other areas seem to be in quite grey areas or have no obvious home. Creating an RDS is likely to be a collaborative effort as we have seen (Chapter 8) so it is probable that a coherent set of training across these different groups is needed.

Exploring further
You might want to go back to the exercise in Chapter 8 to think more about who should lead on training.

Step 4: How should the training be delivered?

Again there are a wide range of plausible options:

- informal discussions
- multi-day workshops
- one-day workshops
- two-hour workshops
- 30-minute bite-sized or twilight sessions
- 15-minute sessions embedded in general researcher training, including induction
- drop-in sessions
- one-to-one consultations
- online tutorials
- panels and presentations
- printed/web based hand-outs/guides
- webinars and lecture recordings
- embedded in research methods training for students
- embedded in induction or research ethics and integrity training for staff.

Any programme of training is likely to incorporate elements of all of these approaches. At the most basic level, researchers can be offered access to webinars and lecture recordings, online tutorials, and guides for just-in-time support and self-learning. This could work well for relatively simple topics like data citation. Where there is quite a complex area where researchers need to develop skills, such as funder requirements or writing data management plans, part-day workshops seem appropriate. Similarly, hands-on sessions with specific tools probably need to be in the form of longer workshops. To deal with complex emergent areas of discussion, such as the management and sharing of sensitive data, some sort of expert panel seems to be an appropriate format. It may be that there are resources to offer researchers one-to-one support to discuss issues in their project.

If the audience is students at any level, then embedding learning in an existing curriculum, preferably with some assessment task linked to it, would be ideal. For staff, embedding something in induction processes is important. Another approach is to link RDM training to training on research ethics and integrity. Researchers know ethics are important and are more likely to attend such sessions. There are strong links between some aspects of RDM and research ethics, e.g. as it relates to handling of sensitive data.

Making and re-using educational resources

It is not necessary to start developing teaching materials from scratch. Open educational resources (OERs) for teaching RDM already exist. While these are not necessarily easy to find, because there is no one repository for OERs, they are worth searching for. Even if they only give you some inspiration, they can be useful for developing learning material for particular disciplines. One such resource is RDMRose, a complete guide to RDM for librarians developed by the authors of this book. It can be accessed from www.sheffield.ac.uk/is/research/projects/rdmrose.

You might well want to openly share your own learning resources that you develop for your teaching.

Step 5: How is the training to be made engaging?

Returning to the issue we posed in the 'Exploring further' section at the beginning of the chapter, it is worth spending time thinking how to make such training as engaging as possible. A number of potential strategies seem to be available:

- Where it is possible, when using more interactive channels, starting with participating researchers' own projects helps ground the debate in the experience of participants. Discussion-based workshops benefit from the ability to connect to individuals' immediate interests.
- Working with real-world case study material again makes for a more realistic experience.
- Learning about RDM can also be linked to employability. For example, RDM-related skills can be mapped to Vitae's Research Development Framework, a model of skills PhD students can learn (www.vitae.ac.uk/researchers-professional-development/about-the-vitae-researcher-development-framework). Another link you could make is to institutional statements about identity. Many institutions have tried to articulate what a graduate or member of staff should be like. Linking into these wider statements brings out the generic value of RDM skills.

Step 6: Evaluating training

There are a number of ways of evaluating training. A very simple approach is simple counting: how many people attended sessions; how many times a webcast was downloaded. Another simple approach is a face evaluation of the quality of the learning materials, perhaps in terms of whether they meet standards of learning material design, e.g. if they have formally stated learning outcomes. Another familiar way to evaluate training is through satisfaction, e.g. through scoring, using feedback forms. This may not be the most reliable way of testing whether people learned what they needed to know, however.

In theory one could test whether people have actually learned from the training by measuring knowledge before and after the session. So some sort of test of skills at the end will be a good indication of whether people understand what was being taught. Of course people may already have knowledge of the topic before the course, so this is not necessarily a test of the learning itself. In most continuing professional development (CPD) such form of examination would not be expected; but if RDM teaching were embedded in a teaching programme it would motivate students a lot more if their course evaluation involved some demonstration of their current knowledge. In the CPD context, the tutor should get a good feel for whether participants have really learned from what they have been exposed to if the session includes practical tasks, e.g. to start writing a research data management plan.

Getting the right mix
Deciding what the key target audiences are, what training to offer them, and how to deliver it, combined with issues around the timing and location of sessions, make designing an effective training programme a non-trivial task. Some other challenges in designing training are:

- Researchers will sign up to a lunchtime session, but will they actually attend?
- If they attend a general hands-on session, will it be possible to adapt the content to their specific needs, so that they learn what they need at their point in their project?
- They may be downloading online training, but are they understanding it?
- How can 1:1 support be offered in any scalable way?
- How do we make RDM a really engaging topic?
- How do we bring together different groups with expertise to deliver the training?

Part of the solution to these conundrums is to offer a range of training based on in-depth analysis of demand and need in different faculties.

Attendance, if not interest will be increased by embedding RDM training in other training, such as for staff in induction or as part of research ethics training, or for students at different levels in research methods courses.

Exploring further

Suppose you were given the responsibility to create a plan for training in a large research intensive institution. Think through the six steps defined above for this imaginary scenario. Given limited resources, how would you try to balance:

- training for senior researchers with direct responsibility for data in large projects versus PhD students
- an online training course that could be taken at any time versus a well developed in-depth course embedded in training for early career researchers
- focusing on a few departments that already recognise the issue versus raising awareness in less aware departments
- having all the training conducted by one individual (based in the library, perhaps) versus bringing together a team from across different support departments.

Further reading

Useful readings about what data literacy is and how it could be incorporated into information literacy are:

Calzada Prado, J. and Marzal, M. Á. (2013) Incorporating Data Literacy into Information Literacy Programs: Core competencies and contents, *Libri*, **63** (2), 123–34.

Carlson, J. and Johnston, L. (eds) (2015) *Data Information Literacy*, Purdue University Press.

CHAPTER 16

Infrastructure for research data storage and preservation

Aims

The aim of this chapter is to outline the infrastructure required for RDM, particularly a repository for sharing data. This is as much about processes and policies as technologies.

Technical infrastructure

Developing and maintaining a technical infrastructure to support research data management is not the goal of institutional RDM, but it is a significant means to achieve the kind of behavioural change that is likely to be the real objective. It does this by enabling researchers to plan their data management from the start of a project, to look after their primary research data whilst they are working on a project, and to support the long-term preservation and sharing of those data. Each stage of this cycle may have its dedicated supporting technical infrastructure, for example:

- an online data management planning tool
- a means for the secure storage of primary research data whilst the project is ongoing, giving access to those who need it, thus facilitating the sharing of data amongst a project team
- and finally, a facility to store data for long-term preservation and, where possible, to share those data with the wider community.

Again, although repository (including preservation and sharing) systems have often been the focus of research data management projects, it is important to realise that they really are only the end point, where a selection of the primary research data produced by a research project will find a permanent home, for example at the point of publication or when the project is wrapped up. This chapter focuses on this end point: a repository for long-term preservation and data sharing.

The repository

A repository is likely to have three components:

1 a catalogue
2 physical storage
3 file format preservation.

The catalogue and storage functionality are part and parcel of any repository solution, yet in some circumstances an institution may only need a catalogue of assets, and may not prioritise preservation. In some cases it may be worth investing in separate software that manages long-term preservation of the data files by monitoring the file formats that are in use, assessing their obsolescence and facilitating their migration to other file formats when needed. Institutions that do not have such a system in place will also need to monitor the file formats in their repository manually, or adopt a preservation policy that explicitly excludes file format migration and does not assure the long-term accessibility of the files in the system.

The lifecycle of a repository for digital information is authoritatively described by the Open Archival Information System (OAIS) reference model (ISO Standard 14721, 2012). This model outlines how data is created by 'producers' and then 'ingested' into the repository system. 'Consumers' are then able to query the system and get 'access' to the data they need. In between, data are stored for the long term, and their preservation is carefully planned and managed. If we follow this three-stage model, moving from producer and ingest via archival management to providing access to the consumer, someone involved in running a research data repository would likely be involved in a wide range of activities, as described in Table 16.1.

Table 16.1 *Supporting preservation*

OAIS entity	OAIS function		Repository manager's activities
Producer	*Ingest*	1	Support academics in choosing and preparing data for preserving and sharing
		2	Ingest data into the repository
Management	*Archival storage and preservation*	3	Monitor file format obsolescence
Consumer	*Access*	4	Handle access restrictions

To expand on the roles identified in Table 16.1:

1 Supporting producers to prepare their data for long-term preservation and data sharing is an important aspect of repository work. It includes ensuring that researchers understand what is expected when they deposit their data. This includes any expectations around metadata, acceptable file formats for long-term preservation, and standards for documentation. Researchers may also need support in choosing what data to select for data preservation and sharing, and any licences and restrictions on access to the data by third parties.
2 The actual process of ingest, where the repository manager processes the data and metadata before it is added to the system, is often much easier.
3 Monitoring file format obsolescence and possibly migrating data files to different file formats can be a process trusted to a software package, such as Preservica (https://preservica.com) or Archivematica (www.archivematica.org), or conducted manually.
4 Finally, giving access to the data via a data catalogue, and handling any access restrictions, fulfils the ultimate purpose of a repository to share usable data. It is often said that the aim is to make data FAIR, that is: Findable, Accessible, Interoperable (e.g. it can be combined with other data) and Re-usable (see Chapter 5 for a discussion of the FAIR principles).

Selecting data for deposit

In all likelihood, not all primary data created in a research project will need to be preserved for the long term. Much of the data that is being produced may not be useful to others. There is a cost associated with keeping material because all data that are selected for long-term preservation need to be structured and documented in such a way that they remain accessible and usable by others in the future. This is a time-consuming process. Furthermore, physical storage has a cost; as does the management work in ensuring preservation. This implies the need to select which data to preserve.

Appraising what data to keep is a process of determining significance. The kinds of question that will be asked at this point are:

• What uses could the data have?

- What data is required to be kept because of policies and regulations?
- What data should be kept because it has a long-term value?

Let's dive a little deeper into these questions.

First of all, datasets can be defined by the purpose for keeping them. If the dataset supports research outputs such as journal articles, PhD theses, and patent applications it may need to be preserved for the purpose of allowing full scrutiny of the research outputs. In this case the data to be preserved should only be the data that were used to reach the conclusions in the research output and any additional data that are required to replicate the reported study findings in their entirety. This is the replication standard.

On the other hand, the data may also be preserved to allow further analysis, because the data are considered to be of long-term value and could be useful to other researchers at some point in the future. In this case, it may very well be that the preserved data items are the raw primary data that were collected or created, though probably a version after initial data quality checks were made.

There are also policies and regulations to consider, as they may require a repository to keep certain data, for example the university's data management policy, records retention schedule, the research funder or sponsor's data management requirements, or data that underpins evaluative reports that could be legally challenged.

Possibly the most interesting question to ask, but also the most difficult one to answer, is the third one, relating to the long-term value of the data. The Digital Curation Centre (2014) has created a short checklist to help determine whether data may be of long-term value:

- Are the data of good enough quality in terms of completeness, sample size, accuracy, validity, reliability or any other criterion relevant in the subject domain?
- Is there likely to be a demand for the data?
- Is it difficult to replicate the data?
- Are the barriers to re-using the data sufficiently low for the intended or likely audience of the research data? For example, do they require proprietary hardware or software to re-use, and if so, how widely used are these in the field of study?

Some of these questions, especially the first, are very difficult to evaluate for the RDM team: it requires subject expertise. The researchers themselves may wish to have the data kept but that may not be a good enough reason. Table 16.2 examines the potential long-term value of different types of data.

Table 16.2 *Some types of data*

Data type	Long-term value
Observational data	Cannot be reproduced because they were based on observing a unique phenomenon or conditions at a particular moment in time, e.g. the state of the polar icecap at a particular date or a survey of a population prior to a major change in circumstances. Potentially a high priority for preservation.
Experimental data	They are captured on equipment in the laboratory and could in theory be reproduced, e.g. gene sequences. Since cost of reproduction could be high there could be some case for preservation.
Compiled data	This is data that has been brought together from other sources. As such it can be reproduced, assuming the original data sources remain accessible. This could be time-consuming and costly but, since it is possible, preservation may be a lower priority.
Simulation data	Created by a computational model, such as a simulation of an economy or a climate. So long as the computer software for the simulation has been kept in a re-usable form, the outputs from any particular running of the model probably do not need to be kept.

Exploring further

If you work for a particular institution that has a data repository look to see if there is a statement of the scope of the collection, such as what types of data are being stored for how long.

If you do not work for an institution with a data repository you could do the same exercise looking at a national or international subject-based or multi-disciplinary research data repository, such as the ones to be found through the Re3data gateway (www.re3data.org/). The Re3data entry for repository gives some links to basic information such as the URL of relevant policies and some of the standards in use.

Many repositories will have specific policies, such as for metadata, data, content, submission and preservation. These constitute a description of the scope and processes for that repository.

Preparing data: metadata and documentation

Preserving research data is pointless if users cannot find them or when they find them cannot understand their potential for further re-use. Re-users not only need to find material that is potentially relevant, they also need to be able to interpret the data, for example understand what units of measurement are being used or how missing values are represented. They also need to understand the circumstances under which the data were collected or created, i.e. insight into the research methodology. It is helpful to think of the replication standard for documentation (King, 1995): researchers should ask themselves what their peers would need to know about their data and how it was collected in order to be able to re-use it in 20 years' time.

Metadata and documentation describing data are therefore vital for any repository that aims to preserve and share research data in the long term. Catalogue metadata ensures discoverability. Methodological documentation ensures usability. In addition, other information may need to be recorded in the repository. This includes, for example, the licence under which the data can be accessed, the funder who paid for the research, and the last time a consumer has downloaded the dataset – a requirement of some research funder policies. There may also be a need for discipline specific information to properly document highly specialised data.

However, a single, common metadata standard for use in research data repositories has not yet emerged. Many universities are creating their own repository solutions with their own approach to metadata. Existing generic repositories, such as Figshare, use their own metadata schema. And the DOI registry service for research data, DataCite, is actively maintaining its own generic metadata standard to describe scholarly data.

It may be useful to think of metadata schemas for research data as having three levels:

1 minimal metadata to enable basic discovery and access, such as fields for the Creator, Title, Publisher, Date, Embargo term, Licence and other access terms and conditions
2 general contextual metadata that may be of an administrative nature (Funder, Grant number, Date of last access) or relate to the methodologies used in the generation of the data (Project information, Data generation process, Geographical location of data collection, Date range of data collection)

3 discipline-specific metadata to enable re-use.

The last category, discipline-specific metadata, could include things such as machine settings and experimental conditions, but this is usually information that is difficult to capture in structured metadata fields. It is therefore useful to distinguish metadata from documentation. Metadata are highly structured data laid out in fields, often with controlled vocabularies in each field. In contrast, documentation can be less structured and is either embedded in a data file (such as in descriptive columns in a spreadsheet) or in an external text file (for example to explain the context within which the data were collected and how missing values are dealt with).

The UK Data Archive, a national centre of expertise in data archiving in the UK, makes a helpful distinction between study-level data documentation, which documents research design and data collection methods, and data-level documentation, which provides documentation at the level of variables in a database or individual objects such as interview transcripts. Study-level documentation can often best be accommodated in separate text files, while data-level documentation is usually embedded in the data files themselves.

Documentation and discipline-specific metadata are important to consider. Most researchers will be familiar with discovery metadata. After all, they are familiar with this from library catalogues and discovery databases such as Scopus and Web of Science. However, documentation and metadata for re-usability of primary data are probably relatively unfamiliar, but that will require the academic's close attention and disciplinary expertise. An RDM metadata specialist is not likely nor expected to understand the myriad of metadata standards in a wide variety of disciplinary fields or to decide which standards may apply to a particular research project.

Although the researcher's input is essential, not all academic colleagues will be willing to commit the time and effort to create extensive metadata and documentation. And the repository manager may not want to exclude datasets from the repository even if they are not fully documented. There are different approaches to a repository's metadata requirements that balance the needs of future users with the level of engagement of data creators:

- minimal requirements to foster as much engagement with as low a threshold as possible but with the risk of low-quality metadata
- maximal requirements to emphasise the need for high-quality metadata to aid discovery and re-use potential and longevity
- a mixed approach depending on the project's needs and the likely interest in the project's data.

Preparing data: file formats

File formats may be inaccessible to others who don't have the appropriate software – for example, file formats used by instruments to log measurements – or they may be linked to software packages from particular vendors. If these vendors go out of business and the file formats become obsolete, how will future researchers be able to access the information? To deal with this issue it is therefore important to accommodate file formats that ensure the longevity of the data, and to have processes in place to deal with situations where file formats in your repository are on the verge of obsolescence.

File formats with the best longevity are typically file formats that are open instead of proprietary, or formats that are considered an industry standard and are therefore likely to be accessible for a long time, for example Microsoft Word, Excel and SPSS. The UK Data Service maintains a list of recommended formats for long-term preservation.

Ingest

Once decisions have been made about the data that needs to be preserved, how the data are documented, and under what conditions they can be made available to the public, the time has come to actually ingest the data files and the accompanying metadata into the repository system. There are a number of things that will be on every checklist at this stage:

- assigning a persistent identifier (such as a DOI) to the dataset
- checking that all files can be opened and that the data does not contain malware or any known viruses
- checking and/or creating metadata and documentation
- creating fixity values (checksums) if the repository software does not do this automatically; this is a way to monitor whether a file is intact or been corrupted

- migrating data to a different file format that ensures better longevity and accessibility
- ensuring that any information about access restrictions is clearly articulated and enforceable.

Exploring further

Continue exploring in a data repository by finding a dataset that you find interesting. You could also try doing this through a search through Datacite, https://search.datacite.org/, though this includes more than just datasets.

Look closely at the metadata and documentation associated with the dataset: are there gaps in the metadata, such as lack of ORCIDs for authors? How full are the metadata, e.g. the subject description? How much additional documentation is supplied?

You may want to download a dataset just to get a feel for what this process is like and try and make an assessment about how re-usable the data might be.

Providing access to consumers

There is an emerging consensus that ideally primary research data should be made available as openly as possible. But when data are sensitive or confidential, there may have to be restrictions to data sharing that necessitate some form of access control. This may, for example, be the case when research participants have not been asked for consent to share their data, when the data underpins a patent, or when there are contractual restrictions to data sharing stipulated by the funder or sponsor of the research. In those cases, it is advisable to explore the extent to which the information can be shared rather than restricting access under all circumstances.

In theory, access controls can be applied to:

- when data can be accessed, for example after an embargo period to allow the creators to publish their findings before the data are released more widely
- who can access the data
- what consumers are allowed to do with the data. This could be restricted through a non-disclosure agreement which would allow the consumer to check any publications based on the data but not to use the data for any new research. Or it could disallow the consumer

from disseminating any information that identifies individuals or attempting to use the data to identify individuals.
• how long the data are available for.

Some data archives run a service that allows 'controlled access' to data by requiring that all data users must be trained and accredited and that they can only access the data in a special secure environment. Individual universities may not be able to set up something as complex as controlled data access in this way, but providing a form of 'safeguarded data access' via nondisclosure agreements or similar understandings is something that can be considered.

Any type of access control has consequences for those who are managing the service:

• The type of access control that is required needs to be established at the point of ingest. Is there a process of approval required for access control?
• Is the act of approving access to a dataset controlled by the creator, or is this task delegated to repository staff? And if so, do repository staff have adequate information to base any decisions on? And if not, what happens when the academic leaves the university?

Exploring further

Imagine you are a researcher about to commence a new project. Decide on a subject field this researcher might be working in, that you know a little about. How easy do you think it would be to decide whether there was existing re-usable data available? From the work you have already done exploring further in this chapter, it should be clear that simply finding a relevant repository could be hard, unless there is a well-established subject repository. One could search through Datacite, but that is quite a simple search. One might also know through a reading of the literature. But at the time of writing the infrastructure simply does not yet exist to discover content, especially that in institutional repositories.

What type of help do you think could be offered by the RDS?

Now imagine you are a researcher nearing the end of the project. How easy would it be to understand the requirements for depositing data? Re-read the repository policy material that you found earlier – is this self-explanatory? How can the researcher be helped to understand the requirements?

Further reading

A useful paper comparing platforms of data repositories is:

Amorim, R. C., Castro, J. A., da Silva, J. R. and Ribeiro, C. (2017) A Comparison of Research Data Management Platforms: Architecture, flexible metadata and interoperability, *Universal Access in the Information Society*, **16** (4), 851–62.

The following paper gives an overview of the design of Re3data:

Pampel, H., Vierkant, P., Scholze, F., Bertelmann, R., Kindling, M., Klump, J., Goebelbecker, H. J., Gundlach, J., Schirmbacher, P. and Dierolf, U. (2013) Making Research Data Repositories Visible: The re3data.org registry, *PLOS ONE*, **8** (11), p.e78080.

References

Digital Curation Centre (2014) Five steps to decide what data to keep: A checklist for appraising research data v.1, Edinburgh: Digital Curation Centre, www.dcc.ac.uk/resources/how-guides.

ISO (2012) *Space Data and Information Transfer Systems – Open Archival Information System (OAIS) – reference model*, ISO Standard 14721:2012.

King, G. (1995) Replication, Replication, *PS: Political Science and Politics*, **28**, 444–52.

CHAPTER 17

Evaluation of RDS

Aims

The purpose of this chapter is to consider how to evaluate RDS and RDM.

Introduction

Evaluation is a controversial topic. On the one hand, it feels obvious that without clearly defined objectives it is impossible to say whether a set of activities are worthwhile. And if we do not collect some data about how we are performing against those objectives we do not know how well we are performing. Tools like SMART objectives reflect this thinking and encourage us to measure whether objectives have been met. At the same time, it may be difficult to define purposes, especially where complex, intangible values are being pursued. In such a context defining our purposes and defining valid measures, i.e. ones that actually measure what we want to achieve, are hard. Capturing data about our achievements, especially quantitative data, is likely to be problematic. At some point more complex measures break down because they are hard to collect and understand.

In the library world, for example, there is pressure to demonstrate the value of the library to student learning. But learning is such a complex construct that it is hard to see how it could ever easily be measured, in a totally valid way. Tools such as the LibQual survey, while widely used in libraries to measure service performance, only compare satisfaction against expectation, not learning itself. Other types of measure, such as the number of resources or even downloads, do not directly link to learning, only the levels of activity.

In addition, the question of evaluation has resonances with the debate around the new public management and neo-liberalisation (see Chapter 5). For many, the way that academia is increasingly run like a private organisation with crude quantitative measures of performance – 'key performance indicators' – erodes the university's true purpose to promote learning and research in their widest sense.

Nevertheless, it would be odd not to write about the evaluation of RDS/RDM here, even though the literature on the topic is actually surprisingly sparse. From a management perspective it makes sense to collect data about performance, even if it is purely for internal consumption within the RDS team. It is highly likely that at some point the RDS will have to demonstrate its value to the rest of the organisation; at that point defining sensible measures of progress will become important.

Exploring further

Go back to Chapter 7 and think about the work you did on the mission of an RDS. Some of the statements were:

- 'To ensure compliance with the mandates of national and international funders of research.'
- 'To create a culture of sharing of research data within institutional research communities.'
- 'To ensure that researchers have access to timely advice and support to meet their needs for RDM.'
- 'To ensure all researchers have a well formulated and actively maintained data management plan.'
- 'To ensure that researchers understand their responsibilities arising around RDM and are trained in the necessary skills.'
- 'To ensure data produced by university of X's research is widely visible.'
- 'To provide a robust and supportive infrastructure for storing, sharing and preserving research data.'

This selection captures some of the main drivers for RDM and also mirrors the different aspects of the RDS that we have been exploring in the last few chapters. These are still quite high-level objectives. If one were to start thinking about evaluating success against these aims, one would want to develop some more specific and time-limited objectives. One could use the SMART concept to try and ensure that they are: Specific, Measurable, Achievable, Realistic and Timely. Give some thought to more SMART objectives in some of the areas.

Principles of evaluation

Once some fairly specific aims have been identified, one can move to the point of evaluating progress against those objectives. A good starting point would be to reflect on the basic principles of evaluation. We can say that evaluation measures should be:

- simple and understandable – given that they may be viewed by a variety of stakeholders, it makes sense if measures are understandable to all parties
- timely – measures of performance that arrive too late to be actionable have limited use
- cost effective to collect – it defeats the point of measuring performance if a lot of resources are expended in collecting measurements
- objective – if possible measures should be seen as 'objective' in the sense that they cannot be manipulated
- benchmarked – some comparators need to be available to establish a standard for what is success or failure
- valid – they must measure the thing that we seek to measure.

As the opening of the chapter suggested, there are some contradictory elements within these principles. Measures of performance can be efficient to collect, easy to understand and timely if they are simple. But simple measures can fail by the criteria of validity. They measure some aspect of performance, but not those one truly wishes to measure. Validity is key, because we do not want to be distracted into measures that are not really measuring what we want to achieve. Yet simple measures are unlikely to be able to capture whether the service is progressing towards its ultimate goals, if those are complex.

We might also want to take into consideration three other factors. Firstly, would we wish to differentiate the performance of the RDS and institutional performance at RDM? The performance of the RDS could be things like how effective the website or training programme is. However, what we are really concerned about is whether researchers themselves are doing RDM well across the institution. Secondly, we could consider if there are different levels of evaluation: for the RDS as a whole or for some particular part of the service, e.g. the website or training. So what are we evaluating, and why? A third consideration is alignment. The objectives of the RDS are nested within wider institutional goals. What are these and how are they being measured? We would want to think about how the RDS contributes in a wider context.

There are also a wide range of ways of collecting evaluation data:

- **Web log data** are relatively easy to collect and 'objective' (barring issues such as caching) but hard to be clear about the attitudes and meaning attached to behaviour.
- **Questionnaires** can reach a wide audience but are superficial compared to interviews.
- **Interviews** allow exploration of complex behaviour and attitudes, but are time-consuming to perform with large groups.

Exploring further

Look at the second column of Table 17.1 of 'measures' that could be used to review the performance of the RDS. How far do they measure things that you think would be key objectives? How far would you say they are simple/understandable, timely, cost-effective, objective, benchmarkable and valid measures?

Measuring impact

In Table 17.1 we list potential measures that could be used to review the performance of the RDS. Each measure captures something important, but all have significant limitations by themselves. Broadly, they tie back to some of the key RDS areas.

Table 17.1 *Impact measures*

	Measures	Comments
1	Percentage of respondents to a staff survey who ticked yes to the question 'Are you aware of the institutional research data policy?'	Percentage of respondents to a staff survey who ticked yes to the question 'Are you aware of the institutional research data policy?' Assuming the response rate on the survey is taken into account, it seems reasonable to evaluate the service based on this evidence about awareness. Of course, we may feel that people only ticked yes because they felt they ought to. Simply being aware that there is a policy is scarcely proof that they understand it or acted upon it.

Table 17.1 *Continued*

	Measures	Comments
2	Number of staff responding to a survey that say they believe data sharing benefits science	Number of staff responding to a survey that say they believe data sharing is a good thing. Through advocacy the RDS seeks to produce a positive culture around data sharing. It is easy for staff to agree to positive statements, but of course it is important that it translates into action.
3	In-depth interviews with researchers in one department tracking their changed attitudes to data sharing	In-depth interviews with researchers in one department tracking their changed attitudes to data sharing.
4	Evidence of a decline in risky data practices, e.g. failure to back up data	Evidence of a decline in risky data practices, e.g. failure to back up data. To be specific we probably need to focus on a particular poor data practice. It is hard to see how we can really measure.
5	Direct evidence that researchers' RDM is good and whether it has improved	Direct evidence that researchers' RDM is good and whether it has improved. This sounds like one of the most valid measures we have identified. The problem is, what would such evidence look like?
6	Average turnaround time on queries to the RDM e-mail account	Hits on the RDM website. Hits on the website tell us there is some recognition of the subject, and that people are trying to find out more. It makes sense to track trends in interest, and which pages are popular. This measure needs some benchmark, and it is not directly measuring RDM knowledge.
7	Hits on the RDM website	Average turnaround time on queries to the RDM e-mail account. This reflects the efficiency and customer service mentality of the RDS. It does not tell us anything about whether queries were answered satisfactorily. For that we might want to collect data on satisfaction.
8	Monthly downloads of examples of DMPs on the website	Monthly downloads of examples of DMPs on the website. This could tell us that we have provided the right sort of material. Again, it needs some comparator, beyond trends over time, since it seems unlikely that many people will download such a page even if it is very useful. It is not direct evidence that DMPs are improving.

Table 17.1 *Continued*

	Measures	Comments
9	Proportion of all projects with a DMP	Proportion of all projects with a DMP. This sounds like a valid measure, assuming the DMPs are good-quality, and are kept up to date after the project start. But how would one practicably capture this, unless depositing a DMP is made part of some routine process?
10	An e-mail from a researcher thanking you for help writing a DMP after they got successful funding for US$500,000	An e-mail from a researcher thanking you for help writing a DMP after they got successful funding for US$500,000. While anecdotal the story is suggestive that at least one researcher has benefited from the service. It is always going to be hard to link success of a bid to the quality of the DMP. It is a small part of the proposal and one of the least critical elements. Nevertheless, the relevance and persuasive power of such narratives should not be under-estimated.
11	Hours of training delivered	Hours of training delivered. While not irrelevant, this tells us not how many people have been trained, whether their expectations were satisfied or whether they learned what the RDS wanted them to learn.
12	Hours of training set against staff numbers in different categories of research staff	Hours of training set against staff numbers in different categories of research staff. An improvement on 6, but does not get at learning or even satisfaction.
13	A summary of evaluations completed at the end of training courses by participants	A summary of evaluations completed at the end of training courses by participants. This tells us about satisfaction, which is highly suggestive that participants enjoyed the learning and it is probable that people learned. It does not tell us about the reach of the courses or whether learned.
14	A comparison of the functionality of the data repository with the best-of-breed system	A comparison of the functionality of the data repository with the best-of-breed system. This tells us whether we currently have the best system, though the issue of cost and total cost of ownership needs to be taken into account.

Table 17.1 *Continued*

	Measures	Comments
15	Total searches in the research data repository	Total searches in the research data repository. This is simple and understandable and cost effective to collect. It is indicative of visibility of the repository, which could be an important objective. But it does not tell us whether users found the material they were looking for (assuming it exists). We may also expect more of our downloads to come from searches in other places than from a direct search of the repository.
16	Total downloads from the research data repository	Total downloads from the research data repository. Again this is simple, understandable, cost-effective to collect and timely. Although it does not tell us what the downloads were used for or give us a sense of the spread of usage across the whole collection it is a useful indicator.
17	Total downloads per annum divided by the total cost of ownership of the repository	Total downloads per annum, divided by the total cost of ownership of the repository. This takes us a step further by trying to work out the cost per download. This seems to be an even more valid measure than 16, but it could be hard to estimate the true cost of ownership of the system and it may be very hard to benchmark.
18	Total citations of DOIs issued by the data repository	Total citations of DOIs issued by the data repository. This is a useful measure of whether data is being truly re-used for further research. Just because it was not actually used does not mean it should not have been kept. It ignores data use for other purposes e.g. for replication purposes or teaching.
19	Increased deposits in the research data repository	Increased deposits in the research data repository. Indicative of growing visibility of the repository internally, and evidence of a growing culture of data sharing. Should take into account the growth of number of deposits.

Table 17.1 *Continued*

	Measures	Comments
20	An estimate of the proportion of funded research depositing data into the repository	An estimate of the proportion of funded research depositing data into the repository. Another way of trying to measure the success in creating a culture of sharing or more simply compliance. It may be hard to be sure how much data has been created, of course! Obviously we also want to think about use.
21	A formal evaluation of metadata quality on a sample of records in the repository	A formal evaluation of metadata quality on a sample of records in the repository.
22	Total budget of the RDS	Total budget of the RDS. Surely relevant but clearly in need of a comparator. Should this be the cost of RDS at comparator institutions or other services in the institution? Should this be set against cost saved or some estimate of risks averted?

A balanced scorecard approach

All the measures we have looked at in Table 17.1 have some relevance. Many are simple, understandable and cost-effective to collect. They can measure the performance of particular services:

- We had measures that attempted a high-level evaluation of the changing research data culture (1–5). This might be affected by factors other than the RDS.
- Some measure support, advice and training (6–13).
- Some are measures around the repository (14–21).
- Some of the measures work at the systems level, e.g. 14. Some work more at the content level: 15–17.

One approach to a more convincing evaluation approach would be to take a number of measures in different areas. The balanced scorecard method, widely used in the commercial sector, points to this approach, with measures in four areas:

- **Users** – how do users experience and value the service?
- **Finance** – is the service value for money?

- **Internal process** – are the key functions performed well?
- **Innovation and learning** – how can the service constantly improve?

In the interests of keeping things simple a few indicators in these areas might be designed to give a cost-effective way to evaluate the RDS.

Exploring further

Spend some time thinking about how you might use the balanced scorecard method to evaluate an RDS you know about. What specific questions would you like to ask in each of the four areas?

Maturity models

One way of performing evaluation that has been widely discussed in the RDM area is the notion of the maturity model. This consists of tools to support a systematic self-assessment of progress in terms of policies, systems, and data culture by comparing the institution against statements that describe different levels of achievement: from a basic level or typical-of-early-days level of RDM through to RDM as 'business as usual' or even best practice.

Some models are for institutions (or parts of institutions, such as libraries), others are for research communities, e.g. the Community Capability Model Framework (Lyon et al., 2012) which defines maturity for data-intensive science. Rather advanced tools exist for some models to be used for organisational self-assessment, such as the CARDIO model (http://cardio.dcc.ac.uk/about).

A maturity model should not really assume one size fits all: the very word 'maturity' tends to suggest that all aspire to the same, high level of service provision or institutional awareness. In fact, for a less research-intensive institution, a relatively low level of 'maturity' may be entirely appropriate. We could use the term 'commitment' rather than 'maturity' to reflect the validity of differing levels of prioritisation of RDM.

A maturity model based around the structure of this book might look something like Table 17.2 on the next page. We suggest for a non-research intensive institution an intermediate commitment where only some departments are heavily invested.

Table 17.2 *Maturity model for evaluation of RDS*

	Low commitment	Intermediate	High commitment
Awareness	Low recognition of RDM as a term, with relevant issues tending to be subsumed under other topics.	Some departments recognise RDM as a priority for themselves and have begun to think through the issues in their area. Recognised in specific or time-limited initiatives.	Widespread understanding of the issues around RDM.
Leadership	Differing voices are heard, some of which argue that RDM should not be an institutional priority. Reactive or wait-and-see stance.	Some patches of strong commitment to particular issues around RDM, but no attempt to make this consistent across every department.	The institution has a clear direction of travel, co-ordinated across institutional services and departmental activity. The institution proactively examines the environment for new developments.
Governance	Little awareness of funder policy among senior management. No specific institutional policy.	Position of some funders understood, e.g. where they are key to funding for that institution. Institutional policy is in place but stress is on individual researcher responsibilities and policy is only reflected in a proscribed range of services.	There is understanding of the wider policy landscape and an up-to-date and widely understood institutional policy, cross-referenced in other policies and supported by well established services. RDS embedded into institutional consultation mechanisms.
Funding	No funding is available to researchers for RDM or for RDS.	Short-term project funding available to support particular initiatives.	Costs and benefits of RDS fully understood and a business plan for a sustainable RDS exists.

Table 17.2 *Continued*

	Low commitment	Intermediate	High commitment
Information	Little attempt to map what is going on within the institution.	Some data about researcher attitudes and behaviour are gathered, but no attempt to be systematic or make sure this is up to date.	Pattern of researcher behaviour well understood, through continuous data collection.
Support and advice	No coherent support across the institution. Reliance on the expertise of a few individuals.	Reliance on generic advice on website. Support confined to particular stages in the research lifecycle, e.g. at the end-of-project stage.	Researchers know where to turn to for support and well developed documentation available. A suitably trained group of staff exists to support RDM.
Data management planning	Only funded projects have DMPs.	DMP concept understood but applied selectively to major projects with a plan for data sharing.	DMPs accepted as a usual require-ment for any project. DMPs are active documents updated through-out the whole project. Quality of DMPs monitored centrally.
Training	No explicit training programme provided.	Training for some areas of research in place.	Training in place for all levels of staff, including at induction and tailored to different research disciplines.
Technological infrastructure	Reliance on project by project or department by department solutions to data storage. No repository in place, reliance on generic subject repositories.	Some departments have infrastructure to support secure storage. Data catalogue in place or small repository.	Appropriate mech-anisms are in place to store active data securely. A repository is in place with robust appraisal system, linked into wider discovery networks and preservation strategy.

Table 17.2 *Continued*

	Low commitment	Intermediate	High commitment
Culture of data sharing and re-use	Data-sharing practices individualistic, confined to certain projects.	Some departments are actively engaged in data sharing and engaged with wider developments.	Wide understanding of the issues, with an assumption of data sharing, even open data, though with appropriate acknowledgement of exceptions. Data recognised as a legitimate output in their own right and data sharing recognised and rewarded.
Evaluation	None undertaken.	Particular projects or initiatives are evaluated on their own terms.	Agreed standards of performance both for researchers and RDS are gathered and regularly published.

Exploring further

Using the structure presented in Table 17.2 attempt to review the level of commitment of an institution you know about.

Reflecting on what insight this exercise gave, consider whether the table could be improved, either by adding more rows to capture performance around a particular area or more columns to reflect a wider range of levels of commitment.

Further reading

Cox, A. M., Kennan, M. A., Lyon, L. and Pinfield, S. (2017) Developments in Research Data Management in Academic Libraries: Towards an understanding of research data service maturity, *Journal of the Association for Information Science and Technology*, **68** (9), 2182–2200.

References

Lyon, L., Ball, A., Duke, M. and Day, M. (2012) Developing a Community Capability Model Framework for Data-Intensive Research, in *Proceedings of*

the 9th International Conference on the Preservation of Digital Objects,
9–16, http://opus.bath.ac.uk/34872/.

CHAPTER 18

Ethics and research data services

Aims

The aim of this chapter is to consider the ethical dimensions of work in RDM.

An ethical service

Like any area of professional work, RDM has its ethical basis and its own ethical dilemmas and challenges.

Many who work in the area of RDM are driven by a strong belief in the benefits of data sharing (or even open data) and its ability to improve science through replicability or transparency and the possibility of new research. Others are motivated by a simpler (but also ethical) desire to do good by providing an excellent service to research communities or by contributing to learning. Others have more pragmatic, less ethically based motives.

Whatever the basis for our belief in the importance of RDM, we should always ask questions about the demands being made on researchers by institutions and governments, and our own role in potentially enforcing these. Open data sounds like an inherently good thing. But there is the potential for it to be used as a means to disadvantage particular types of research, such as qualitative research, where gaining consent for re-use may in some cases affect participation rates negatively. It also has the potential to be used by senior academics to appropriate the work of more junior colleagues. This reflects the fact that any agenda can and will be used politically within a nexus of power in an organisation. More generally there may be systematic connections between the agenda to share data and control over research. Such issues of power relate to local situations within departments; equally they exist in the imbalance between Western institutions and in developing countries. Open access, especially gold open access – where the publisher makes the final published version openly available on their web site – seems to actually disadvantage developing countries. We should always be asking critical questions about equity and justice within digital scholarship.

Exploring further
What is the moral purpose of RDM for you? Do you see any tensions with other values that you hold? For example, do you see any conflicts between best practices in managing data and the need for researchers to have autonomy and freedom to do research as they believe is best? Are there potential conflicts around beliefs about who owns data?

Research ethics

There is also a strong link between the role of RDM and wider ethical issues around research, especially where research involves human subjects and so issues of consent, privacy and anonymity. A basic principle of ethical research is that the subjects give informed voluntary consent to their participation. It is vital that participants understand to what they are consenting, with an awareness of the likely implications. However, this becomes more problematic when consent is being asked for unknown uses in the future. If researchers feel that asking for this kind of consent could affect response rates or skew responses towards certain groups, it could even be that it affects the validity of research.

Often in research based on human subjects it is promised that subjects' identities will be effectively protected through anonymisation. Good RDM will ensure that people participating in research do have their privacy protected, e.g. by avoiding data breaches. But data sharing does increase some types of risk. In sharing data more widely, anonymisation practices have to be rigorous. Part of the quality checks undertaken on new deposits might have to be on how effectively anonymisation has been performed. This goes beyond simply removing personal names and addresses from a file. The rush to open data does create new types of vulnerabilities, especially for data that could potentially be mined and then combined with other sources to identify individuals. It is more likely that the burden of care lies with the researcher than the repository, but it is clearly part of the role of the repository to remind researchers of their responsibilities.

Many researchers also have ethical concerns about how data they share might be re-used: will they be understood? Will they be used in beneficial ways or could it be exploited for commercial benefit, when that was not the original intent? Structures to govern how data are re-used need to reflect such concerns.

These issues are primarily for researchers to be concerned with, but the RDS needs to show respect for such concerns and be thinking about how the infrastructure can assist rather than degrade such protections. No infrastructure is politically or value neutral.

Exploring further
What would be your responses to the following statements?

- 'Sharing research data openly creates new risks to human subjects: there is no need to take such risk.'
- 'Human subjects give their time to research out of public spirit; it follows that the greatest use should be made of the data created from working with them.'
- 'It is hard to get people to participate in this research. Why should I risk affecting participation by placing more requirements on participants by asking them to allow their data to be re-used?'
- 'My ethics committee are not familiar with research data sharing. For that reason it is not worth the risk of including data sharing as part of the consent process.'
- 'The cost of anonymising this data outweighs the potential value in re-use.'

Dilemmas for RDS

The ethical principles of particular professional groups involved in supporting RDM draw attention to fundamental dilemmas about information access. For example, in defining core library values there is a need to balance issues around access, intellectual freedom and intellectual property. Consider the ethical principles of the American Library Association:

I. We provide the highest level of service to all library users through appropriate and usefully organized resources; equitable service policies; equitable access; and accurate, unbiased, and courteous responses to all requests.

II. We uphold the principles of intellectual freedom and resist all efforts to censor library resources.

III. We protect each library user's right to privacy and confidentiality with respect to information sought or received and resources consulted, borrowed, acquired or transmitted.

IV. We respect intellectual property rights and advocate balance between the interests of information users and rights holders.

(American Library Association, www.ala.org/tools/ethics)

All these principles feel relevant to RDM, but pull in somewhat different directions. The ethos of promoting equal access, for example, can cut against the principle of protecting the rights of those creating information. There are always dilemmas between principles such as open access, the rights of those creating information, and resource availability. Those who make the effort to create material must be the primary beneficiaries of the effort, though the rights of those who fund that effort should also be considered. Open access has a resource cost, so implies using resources that could also be used for other worthy ends.

Exploring further
There are also dilemmas around freedom of expression. What if research conducted by or sponsored by a tobacco company were offered for deposit? It would be hard to differentiate between neutral research and research that was conducted to promote a cause we might disagree with. However, would refusing to take the data be a form of censorship? Should such considerations come into appraisal decisions around data?

Ethics in professional relationships
As in any area of professional practice, RDM poses day-to-day ethical challenges around professional relationships, including issues of equity and diversity. These would encompass:

- Respect for colleagues and other professionals. RDM is inherently about working with people with other expertise, be that in doing research or supporting it. Ethical relationships are a key foundation for the necessary trust. There could be issues around:
  - respecting researchers' concerns about opening up their data
  - over-claiming for one's own expertise area

- – deciding when to refer or defer to the expertise of others
- – respecting cultural differences that exist between professional groups.
- Impartiality, and not promoting one's personal interests or opinions ahead of service to users.
- Concerns around equity, gender, race, sexual orientation and disability, and how these affect systems, staff and users. For example, are there any issues in access to research data systems arising from these issues? Are there issues around the representation of users? Understanding how one's assumptions can colour a service and affect user responses to it can be hard to unravel. Something as simple as an apparently neutral image of a lab to illustrate the idea of research data can be seen to promote unhelpful stereotypes around the nature of research.
- A commitment to excellent performance and keeping one's professional knowledge up to date.

Exploring further

Look again at some RDM websites: Is there anything in the imagery or wording that you consider potentially unhelpful by promoting stereotypes about researchers?

Further reading

Understanding research ethics from a researcher's point of view is central to understanding some of the challenges to data sharing, particularly in the social sciences.

Corti, L., Van den Eynden, V., Bishop, L. and Woollard, M. (2014) *Managing and Sharing Research Data: A guide to good practice*, Sage.

Exploring further

If you are part of a professional body or thinking of joining one, look at their ethics policies. How do their general principles apply to working in RDM?

CHAPTER 19

A day in the life working in an RDS

Aims

The aim of this chapter is to give you a more vivid sense of what working in RDM is like through a sketch of what this looks like on a day-to-day basis for someone whose main role is RDM.

RDM in practice

There are many roles in a university that engage with research data management. Research administrators prepare grant applications or manage post-award administration that involves RDM. IT professionals manage the hardware and software that our RDM infrastructure uses. A librarian might help a researcher identify suitable datasets for re-use. But there are only a handful of roles where RDM is a substantial part of a job description. Examples are research support librarians, research data management advisors, repository managers, and research data co-ordinators. What this might be like will vary a lot between institutions, depending on their level of commitment to RDM.

In this chapter we explore the daily experience of someone in the role of Research Data Manager. Everyday work with research data management in this role is likely to include three areas:

1 strategic development
2 advocacy, training and support
3 repository and infrastructure management.

Strategic development

Strategic work is the future-oriented aspect of the job. It involves such things as policy development, including keeping the RDM policy up to date, and plans for future service development. It also involves regularly evaluating where you are, for example using a maturity framework or through measuring compliance with funder requirements, or monitoring restrictions to openness of data (See Chapter 17). For example, the *Concordat on Open Data* (discussed in Chapter 5) implies that there needs to be some form of continuous oversight of progress.

Many universities have set up research data management steering groups that bring together stakeholders from throughout the university to give direction to and oversee the establishment and smooth working of research data management services. This has often been in response to funder requirements and other government policy. In this process it is vital that all stakeholders are involved, including academics from all faculties. As we have seen, buy-in from influencers is important but not guaranteed – especially in the arts and humanities, where the perceived absence of data gives rise to the feeling that research data management does not apply.

Measuring compliance is part of strategic development, as it will inform the effectiveness of the service and its future shape. This can be particularly challenging. How to gauge whether a piece of research produces data or not, or whether the data included in any supplementary materials in a journal article are sufficient and comply with funder requirements, is not easy. Apart from the challenging nature of compliance measurement, one can also justifiably question whether this is an appropriate task. People from a library background, in particular, are loathe to get involved in enforcing or monitoring compliance of academics.

It is highly likely that the strategy side of the role will involve developing, designing and running projects, be those to procure and implement a system or more simply to redesign and evaluate a training programme.

In a typical week, the research data manager could find themselves:

- preparing a report for a meeting
- attending meetings
- working on management issues relating to a major developmental project
- reviewing staff work objectives
- desk-researching a new trend that has been identified as of importance.

On a day-to-day basis this aspect of the role is demanding because it involves engaging in quite high-level considerations and trying to influence the course of decision making in the institution. But it should work to a fairly predictable round of regular meetings and responding to deadlines for reports.

Advocacy, training and support

Work in advocacy, training and support is varied and sometimes challenging. Since RDM is a culture change with regards to creating, documenting and sharing data, there are many kinds of barrier to deal with when talking to academics.

Support needs are unpredictable. It is therefore vital that the right help is available for researchers at the right time, just when they need it. This is very difficult to achieve. There is not a clear annual cycle of activity, because research proposals can be written at any time and projects can be starting and finishing throughout the year. In a typical week, the research data manager could find themselves doing any of the following:

- giving presentations for departments and research centres and various university committees about RDM
- attending meetings with individual researchers, mostly to talk about their funder's requirements or about data management plans as part of funding applications
- commenting on submissions to a DMP read-through service
- running workshops for doctoral students, doctoral supervisors and researchers
- updating guidance on the website and in the data management planning tools in use
- collecting further information about RDM awareness and needs, for example through surveys.

Unlike strategic work, a lot of advocacy and support work is reactive and the commonest type of work is likely to be helping with DMPs. Often requests for help in writing DMPs are urgent. Other aspects, like training, are more planned, but even with these an invitation to present for 5 or for 50 minutes can arrive at short notice.

This reflects a major challenge of RDM, that is unfamiliar to most researchers. Finding ways to reach out to researchers and engage them more proactively is challenging. Although one can use a wide variety of channels, including face-to-face presentation, newsletters, messages on plasma screens or e-mails signed by a senior academic with a responsibility for research leadership in the institution, facilitating a culture change will be a long-term process that meets varying amounts of resistance. Younger generations of researchers seem to be more on board than those who have been working in research for a long time and have established habits that are difficult to break.

It also proves challenging to reach out to researchers at the right time. Workshops are inevitably not at the exact time a researcher needs help. This is where the trigger of writing a DMP is useful, because the requirement to write one at the beginning of a research project will bring them to the RDS seeking help. At the point of deposit is another point of engagement, but it is very difficult to get involved in the process in between – where critical work happens during data collection and documentation.

Overall, it may be that compliance is the main driver to undertaking action, though one might want to shift this towards a more positive culture around data sharing. In many cases, researchers deposit their data because they have to and do not want to take the risk of future sanctions. They don't share because they want to share with their peers for re-use. This means minimum engagement, minimum effort and a poor selection of data to be shared and poor documentation. Data management and sharing is clearly an afterthought that is considered to be an administrative burden imposed upon an already extremely busy working life.

It is a common experience that researchers are more receptive to messages around direct benefits of looking after live data – storing, backing up, file-naming conventions – than they are about data sharing and its benefits. This is definitely a way to attract researchers' interest.

When it comes to promoting data sharing, one may want to avoid an emphasis on compliance (even if this does work as a driver) and stress instead the benefits of data preservation and sharing-where-possible, mainly emphasising integrity. One approach that seems to work is to link advocacy closely to ethics procedures, working with our research ethics committees. This potentially puts RDM into the workflow of much research, at least any work involving human subjects (and so subject to ethics review).

Repository work

In a typical week, the RDM manager might find themselves doing all or some of the following:

- Meeting with a developer to discuss deposit workflows and the implementation of a metadata schema:
  - the screens depositors go through, the metadata they are asked to provide, and what fields are compulsory or not
  - this includes dropdowns with controlled vocabulary and how we would register links to our institutional repository for research outputs and register funders.
- Working on the ingestion of new datasets. This can be a time-consuming process if the depositor does not provide sufficient metadata or if they are of a low quality. It sometimes involves going back and forth with the academic to obtain all the information that is needed to create a useful record.
- Quality checking the metadata using shared guidelines with our outputs repository and checking all files for whether they can be opened, are free of viruses and are in an acceptable file format that facilitates long-term conservation.
- Monitoring compliance with any funder requirements.
- Providing an academic with a data availability statement and minting a DOI for the dataset via the DataCite registry.

Much of the work done when checking deposits has to do with the actual data themselves. It is probable that the RDM manager and his team do not understand the data nor can they gauge whether the data are sufficiently documented to be usable by other people in the long term. It is hard to know whether the correct metadata standards have been used to describe the data. This is a challenge but it can be argued that the content of the dataset is irrelevant for this work, as long as the responsibilities of the depositor and the repository are clearly defined. So a typical workflow might look something like this:

1 The principal investigator (PI) prepares the deposit. They select the data that need to be preserved, choose the correct file formats and document the data appropriately. They also create a metadata record in the repository, but are asked to send us the data separately.
2 Once they have received the data, the RDM team check the metadata record. The metadata are checked for completeness and accuracy, using a set of metadata rules that are similar to the ones one would use for our outputs repository. This includes things like

capitalisation and punctuation. There may be a need to liaise with the depositor to supplement or correct metadata.

3 The RDM team would also check for funder compliance regarding any access restrictions. If access is restricted, is sufficient reason given as to why, and are the conditions under which access can be given clearly articulated?

4 The team also check for the presence of malware and viruses, confirm the technical characteristics of the files, and the acceptability of the chosen file formats for long-term preservation.

5 They could then check the packaging in individually downloadable units (some files may be zipped together) and prepare the repository record. Note that the content of the files may not be checked (i.e. for file-level documentation). This is the responsibility of the author.

6 Finally, part of the process is to reserve a DOI according to an established naming schedule and send this DOI to the researcher for use in data citation and data availability statements.

Although the timing of deposit could be unpredictable, checking deposits is likely to be something that can be handled as a routine. Communication is likely to be remote, through e-mail, rather than face to face.

RDM day to day

This chapter has described some typical features of RDM work. Of course, actual experience could be very different, for example if one were specialising in a particular area such as metadata creation in a large institution or were embedded in a research team.

What our snapshot reveals is a complex pattern of demands. Some work is urgent; other work involves long-term thinking. Some is high-level strategy work, demanding a vision and planning and influencing skills. Some is much more mundane, requiring close attention to detail. Some work fits into a clear process, like the repository workflow, other work is very unpredictable, such as DMPs or advocacy. Not surprisingly, communication skills are central to the whole role.

In the next chapter we will think more about the range of skills, knowledge and mindsets that is needed in RDM support work.

Exploring further

Start thinking about what types of knowledge, skills and mindset an RDS seems to need. You may want to start thinking about whether you have these attributes and, if not, how you might develop them. This is discussed more in the next chapter.

CHAPTER 20

Conclusion: the skills and mindset to succeed in RDM

Aims

The aim of this chapter is to reflect on the kind of knowledge, skills and mindsets needed for work in RDM, and how to plan to develop and demonstrate these, and to discuss some starting points for keeping up to date.

Working in RDM

Reflecting on the content of the book, we can begin to say that the knowledge, skills and mindsets that you might have already or will want to develop to work in this field could include the following:

- **An interest in research and a belief in the benefits to society of research.** This implies a willingness to engage with researchers to help them, even if ultimately you may not fully understand what their research is about.
- More specifically it would be valuable to have **an interest in developments in areas such as data handling, data analysis and data visualisation, and in evaluating digital tools that support these activities**.
- **Curiosity, a thoughtful approach and a willingness to learn new things.** You will be the kind of person who wants to go and find out what is going on, be that within your own institution or in others. You are not afraid to deal with complexity or get involved even where professional practices are not well established.
- **Good influencing skills**. Trying to persuade researchers to see the importance and benefits of RDM is a key part of the role. It is a challenging one because of the diversity of research (see Chapter 14).
- **Leadership skills.** In the widest sense you will want to make a difference to your organisation. That implies making some quite

courageous and tenacious stands in order to improve the long-term situation (see Chapter 6).

- **Excellent networking and collaboration skills**. Knowing who is who across the organisation and working with others, disregarding boundaries of formal organisational structures and hierarchies, will be a key challenge. Building good contacts outside the organisation is important too. Throughout the book we urge you to get out of your office and talk to people (e.g. Chapters 8, 14).
- **A service orientation.** An interest in developing services to help people do their own job better (Chapter 7).
- **An interest in developing and promoting policy** (as discussed in Chapter 10).
- **An interest in teaching others**. A big part of RDM will be developing an effective training programme (see Chapter 15).
- **Good organisation and management, including project management, skills.** You will need to be skilful in collecting evidence to support your decisions and designing effective service structures (Chapters 7, 9, 10).
- **Confidence with IT systems**. A lot of RDM is driven by digital technologies. Part of the solution lies in new infrastructural systems, such as to repositories or current research information systems (CRIS). You do not need to be a software engineer, however. You will be a quick learner with IT tools. You will have a sense of what is possible with new systems and be able to talk with confidence to those designing systems (Chapter 16).
- **A knowledge of the principles around data quality, and digital preservation.**
- **A professional, ethical approach** would underlie all this (see Chapter 18).

Maybe you are already highly skilled in all these areas. Taken all in all, these kinds of knowledge, skills and mindset will take you a long way in many roles, not just RDM. The transferable skills mentioned above are increasingly necessary in any more dynamic professional sphere. In an increasingly data-centric world more specialist knowledge, such as that around data management, has a range of other applications too, e.g. most organisations are trying to make better use of data to inform decision making.

Perhaps it is more likely that you have some of the skills and need to assemble a team and network of contacts that give you access to those skills and knowledge.

Your career plan and RDM

Traditional career planning advice often revolves around four aspects that you can yourself control:

Reflective self-awareness is an honest analysis of your strengths, weaknesses and potential. Perhaps you are really good at the people side of RDM, but are not so strong on technical aspects. Your personal development plan needs to reflect this realisation: either mapping out how to get up to speed on some technologies to build your confidence or recognising the weakness and building contacts with others who are good at the technical side of things. Although we do not often talk about it, our professional lives are full of value issues. Where do you stand on open access and research integrity? Why do you care about supporting research? Knowing your own values – and what you are passionate about – is important to energising you in your work. Through reading this book you should have a clearer idea of the issues at stake with RDM.

Opportunity awareness – this is about understanding key developments in the sector and having a sense of its direction of travel. How are RDS developing in comparable institutions? What current shifts in wider policy are under way within the institution that could affect your role? Knowing this will help you understand how your skills and knowledge fit what institutions are looking for. The book and the activities you have done as part of reading it should give you a handle on this. A big part of opportunity awareness happens through the network of people you build, of contacts you want to help (and to help you). Doing some of the activities suggested in the book will help you to establish these sorts of contacts inside an organisation and in other institutions.

Decision making – this is about having short- and long-term plans. You can plan to go on a course to develop some understanding of virtual lab notebooks; developing higher-level coding skills is going to take longer. Having a clear concept of where you want to get to professionally is a condition, though not a guarantee, of success.

Transition skills – change is endemic, we need skills to make the change in ourselves to adjust to a different area of work. We often think in terms of new knowledge or even skills, but moving into RDM probably requires a new mindset too. Hopefully the book has prompted you to have the conversations with people to reveal that to you and help you think consciously about what is required.

These four elements are largely under your control. Of course, the reality of the world is a lot messier than it appears in your draft career plan. There are quite a few elements beyond your control. Indeed, if anything the most important factors are ones that are both beyond your control and unexpected. This implies developing some other character-istics, such as:

Resilience. You can plan to develop some data analysis skills through a course, but just as you are finishing it a new colleague joins your team with expertise in just this area! You need to have the mindset to bounce back and still make the most of the positives in the situation.

'**Luck readiness**'. An opportunity to get involved in a project with researchers comes up. Do you make sure you are on the list of invitees, and when the opportunity comes do you speak up and get noticed? Trying to move out of a more passive and reactive mode is hard if you work in a fairly formal or managed environment. Moving into a dynamic area such as RDM makes more demands on you to find and maximise opportunities. Recognising or making opportunities is a key skill. Asking for mentoring or work shadowing opportunities could really make a big difference to your progress.

So a balance of planning and responsiveness to the environment is called for. Hopefully this book should give you the beginnings of an under-standing of the social world of RDM, its key debates and challenges, and through the activities we have suggested you have begun to participate in it in an active way.

Exploring further

One simple technique for improving your profile is the elevator pitch, a short, punchy explanation of who you are and what you do. You can use it to introduce yourself to people at a meeting or when you meet them first informally. It is really necessary in contexts like RDM, where people are not quite sure what it is about. Just saying 'I am the research data officer' is not very helpful.

An elevator pitch is meant to be put over in a few sentences, as if you bumped into someone in the elevator, and had just enough time to talk to them on a journey between floors. One way to present this is to start by articulating a problem that people have (including whoever you are talking to) and how you can help people solve that problem. An anecdote or story is another good type of hook. Try writing a few sentences that articulate what you have to offer in this form. You will need to try it out and hone the wording to ensure it sounds natural. Here are a few examples of the kind of thing that might make up an elevator pitch:

- 'Have you ever lost track of an important digital file because you cannot remember where you saved it or it got accidentally deleted? My expertise lies in helping researchers make sure that never happens to them!'
- 'Have you ever looked at a piece of research and thought "That is fascinating! I would like to repeat that in my context and compare the results."? But what you need is the underlying data so you can really do the comparison. My job is to get people to share their research data, where they can, so that kind of new research can happen!'
- 'A colleague had their laptop stolen recently. They were pretty careful and everything was encrypted, so thankfully some of the more personal stuff on the computer was not in danger. But there was some working data on there. This had taken months to collect, process and analyse. Luckily I had been talking to them a few weeks before and explained to them about a new storage service. So I guess that is my role, to give researchers that security of knowing how to manage their data.'

On the whole a positive story, rather than a scare story, probably makes the other person feel better about you – but either approach can help others understand the point of what you do. You may feel the exercise is a bit cheesy, but the real power of the exercise is how it prompts you to think about things from an outside perspective: from the point of view of whoever you are talking to rather than your point of view.

In reality you will probably tailor your elevator pitch to who you are talking to, so you might want to consider how you might vary it for different audiences. When you try it out for real the practice will help you say what you want, but should not come out sounding over rehearsed.

Exploring further
As you near the end of the book, now is a good time to pause and think more systematically about how you see the potential to develop your own role in RDM. Some sort of personal audit under the headings identified in

the first section would be useful. What are your strengths and weaknesses in relation to the mindsets described earlier in the chapter? How do you perceive the current opportunities around you? What are your immediate development needs and long-term objective?

Keeping up to date

The challenge and the attraction of RDM is that it is not a solved problem and we do not know what the end point will be. For opportunity awareness you need to deepen your understanding of what is happening around you and keep up-to-date with the latest thinking. The following resource list is a starting point for that.

Key organisations

There are probably some key national organisations in your country that you need to be aware of, such as research funders, as well as those building infrastructure, like data archives. For example, the Australian National Data Service (ANDS) or Jisc in the UK have done a lot of work around RDM. The UK's Digital Curation Centre is also recognised for its excellence around RDM. All three have excellent websites with lots of resources that could be used in any country. Anyone interested in the subject will find their work useful to refer to.

Depending on which subject or subjects you are supporting there will also be professional bodies for academics which may be doing relevant work.

A number of international developments are relevant to every reader of this book, such as:

- Research Data Alliance (rda) (www.rd-alliance.org) is an international organisation promoting open data sharing, with 6000 institutional members.
- International DOI Foundation (www.doi.org) provides unique persistent identifiers for digital objects.
- Datacite (www.datacite.org) is an international body providing DOIs for research data.
- ORCID, https://orcid.org, provides an infrastructure of unique, persistent identifiers for each individual researcher
- Re3data (www.re3data.org) is a gateway to data repositories.
- Repositories include FigShare (http://figshare.com), Dryad 9

(http://datadryad.org), Mendeley Data (https://data.mendeley.com), Zenodo (http://zenodo.org), DataHub (http://datahub.io), DANS (www.dans.knaw.nl), and EUDat (www.eudat.eu)

- Transparency and Openness Promotion (TOP) Guidelines (https://cos.io/our-services/top-guidelines) are a set of standards for publications to define their open access expectations.

Key events

RDM is of increasing interest to a number of professional communities, so there are strands of discussion in a number of domains. More specialist events for those working in RDM include:

- International Digital Curation Conference (www.dcc.ac.uk/events/international-digital-curation-conference-idcc)
- IASSIST – International Association for Social Science Information Services and Technology (www.iassistdata.org/)
- Force11 (future of research and e-scholarship founded in 2011) conference (www.force11.org).

Twitter

Online forums like listservs still have life, but Twitter is used by many RDM professionals. Following key organisations such as those mentioned above is also recommended.

Reading

There is a growing body of studies on research data practices in different disciplines and also on the development of RDS. While far from comprehensive, Bailey's annotated *Research Data Curation Bibliography* is a useful starting point (http://digital-scholarship.org/rdcb/rdcb.htm).

The 'Further reading' sections of previous chapters of the book have identified some of the key works you might want to have on your shelf.

Index